I0092158

DIET OF WORMS

Zapf Chancery Tertiary Level Publications

A Guide to Academic Writing by C. B. Peter (1994)

Africa in the 21st Century by Eric M. Aseka (1996)

Women in Development by Egara Kabaji (1997)

Introducing Social Science: A Guidebook by J. H. van Doorne (2000)

Elementary Statistics by J. H. van Doorne (2001)

Iteso Survival Rites on the Birth of Twins by Festus B. Omusolo (2001)

The Church in the New Millennium: Three Studies in the Acts of the Apostles by John Stott (2002)

Introduction to Philosophy in an African Perspective by Cletus N.Chukwu (2002)

Participatory Monitoring and Evaluation by Francis W. Mulwa and Simon N. Nguluu (2003)

Applied Ethics and HIV/AIDS in Africa by Cletus N. Chukwu (2003)

For God and Humanity: 100 Years of St. Paul's United Theological College Edited by Emily Onyango   (2003)

Establishing and Managing School Libraries and Resource Centres by Margaret Makenzi and Raymond Ongus (2003)

Introduction to the Study of Religion by Nehemiah Nyaundi (2003)

A Guest in God's World: Memories of Madagascar by Patricia McGregor (2004)

Introduction to Critical Thinking by J. Kahiga Kiruki (2004)

Theological Education in Contemporary Africa edited by GrantLeMarquand and Joseph D. Galgalo (2004)

Looking Religion in the Eye edited by Kennedy Onkware (2004)

Computer Programming: Theory and Practice by Gerald Injendi (2005)

Demystifying Participatory Development by Francis W. Mulwa (2005)

Music Education in Kenya: A Historical Perspective by Hellen A. Odwar (2005)

Into the Sunshine: Integrating HIV/AIDS into Ethics Curriculum Edited by Charles Klagba and C. B. Peter (2005)

Integrating HIV/AIDS into Ethics Curriculum: Suggested Modules Edited by Charles Klagba (2005)

Dying Voice (An Anthropological Novel) by Andrew K. Tanui (2006)

Participatory Learning and Action (PLA): A Guide to Best Practice by Enoch Harun Opuka (2006)

Science and Human Values: Essays in Science, Religion, and Modern Ethical Issues edited by Nehemiah Nyaundi and Kennedy Onkware (2006)

Understanding Adolescent Behaviour by Daniel Kasomo (2006)

Students' Handbook for Guidance and Counselling by Daniel Kasomo (2007)

BusinessOrganization and Management: Questions and Answers by Musa O. Nyakora (2007)

Auditing Priniples: A Stuents' Handbook by Musa O. Nyakora (2007)

The Concept of Botho and HIV/AIDS in Botswana edite by Joseph B. R. Gaie and Sana K. MMolai (2007)

DIET OF WORMS
Quality of Catering in Kenyan Prisons

Jacqueline Cheptepkeny Korir
**Lecturer, Department of Hotel and
Hospitality Management, Moi University,
Eldoret Kenya**

Zapf Chancery
Limuru, Kenya

First Published 2011
© Jacqueline Cheptepkeny Korir
All rights reserved.

Cover Concept and Design
C. B. Peter

Associate Designer and Typesetter
Nancy Njeri

Edited by
Charles M. Ngugi, PhD

Publishing Consultant
C. B. Peter

Printed by
Kijabe Printing Press,
P. O. Box 40,
Kijabe.

Published by

Zapf Chancery Publishers Africa Ltd,
C/o St. Paul's University
P. O. Box Private Bag - 00217
Limuru, Kenya.
Email: zapfchancerykenya@yahoo.co.uk
Mobile: 0721-222 311

ISBN 978-9966-1506-6-0

*This book has been printed on
fully recyclable,*

To my beloved husband Kimeli Korir and our
dear children Simbolei Sambor
and Kendagor Chebirir

Abstract

Catering in Kenyan prisons is an issue of much concern to the government and the entire society as it results in an increase in bad health and hardening the behaviour of prisoners. The purpose of the study was to investigate the factors affecting the quality of catering in selected prisons in Kenya. Little or no effort has been done to improve catering in prisons which may have otherwise helped in the rehabilitation of prisoners in Kenya. If the quality of catering in Kenyan prisons is not addressed, opportunities for rehabilitating and integrating prisoners into the mainstream society might be in jeopardy hence the need for the study.

The objective of the study was to investigate the extent to which the type of food served, food preparation and service affect the quality of catering in prisons. In addition, the study sought to verify the extent to which the menu outlined in the "first schedule" stipulated in the Prisons Act Cap 90 was adhered to.

Purposive sampling and simple random sampling were used to select five prisons in Kenya and the research respondents respectively. There are 91 prisons in Kenya with a total population of 44,977 prisoners. The prisons selected were Eldoret men, Ngeria, Eldoret women, Kamiti Maximum and Langata women prisons. The sampling frame comprised of a population of 5,830 prisoners. A sample size of 387 prisoners, 34 prison warders, 5 storekeepers and 5 officers' in-charge of the selected prisons were used in the study. Instruments for collecting primary data included researcher assisted questionnaires, structured interview schedules, participant observation schedules and conversations. Sources of primary data were prisoners, prison warders, storekeepers and officers in charge of the selected prisons. Sources of secondary data were documents, publications, libraries and the internet. The study used both descriptive and inferential statistics to test the data of factors that affect the quality of catering in prisons. Multiple regression, independent samples t-test and one-way ANOVA were used to analyse the data. T-tests were used to test the hypotheses.

Results of the study showed that the quality of catering is poor with an average rate of 2 on a five point likert scale recorded on the low level of satisfaction obtained in quality of catering in prisons. The first three hypothesis tested revealed that all the variables included in the study were statistically significant and therefore were all important in explaining quality of catering in Kenyan prisons. On comparison of the diet served in the prisons against that stipulated in the Prisons Act Cap 90, the two diets, were found to be significantly different from each other. This indicated the fact that what is proposed in the Prisons Act was not what is actually implemented. The results showed that the satisfaction levels between men and women prisons with regards to quality of catering actually differed. The conclusion of the research was that the quality of catering in Kenyan prisons was poor hence, there is need to overhaul and revamp the Prisons catering services.

The researcher recommends that the Kenya Prisons Service Department urgently contract caterers to run the management of catering services in all prisons. In the meantime, prison warders in charge of kitchens should be trained in management of food and thereafter train prisoners working in the kitchens. This may go along way in solving problems such as poor health, spread of disease and eventually creating opportunities for reforming prisoners and social reintegration of prisoners and community protection. The conclusion that the quality of catering services in the selected prisons was poor could be extended to all Kenyan prisons since the sample was assumed to be representative of all the prisons in Kenya.

Acknowledgements

I acknowledge the invaluable scholarly guidance, patience and close supervision of my supervisors Dr. Timothy Sulo and Mr. Sawe Belsoy throughout the entire research. Their immense wisdom, understanding and constructive advice and criticism were a source of great encouragement. Special thanks go to Rose Burugu and all the lecturers of the Hospitality Department and my fellow masters students for their comments during the proposal writing

I am grateful to my beloved husband Kimeli Korir, children Simbolei Sambor and Kendagor Chebirir for their patience and support during my study. I particularly thank my husband for the moral and financial assistance during my entire research. It is worth noting that he was one of my research assistants. I thank my parents and family for their encouragement during the research.

I feel greatly indebted to Kenya Prisons Service Department for making it possible for me to carry out this research. In particular, I feel indebted to the Commissioner of Prisons, Mr. Gilbert Omondi and Dr. John Kibosia, Director of Prisons Health Services for their great inspiration and facilitating my access to the prisons. I am grateful to all the individual officers in charge and warders of Eldoret Men, Ngeria, Eldoret women, Kamiti Maximum and Langata Women's prisons for facilitating the actual data collection and according me adequate security while in the prisons. I am especially thankful to those prisoners who took part in the study, without whose willing co-operation, this research would not have been possible. Special thanks go to Kigen, Michael Chebet, Collins, Grace Onyango, Keino, Maweu, Rose and Charity for their individual support while collecting data at the prisons. I thank the entire prison community for their contribution and hospitality.

I appreciate with gratitude the devotion and dedication provided by my Research Assistants during data collection and analysis. These included Edward Cheruiyot, John Koech, Abraham Chirchir, Titus Kemboi, Rose Burugu, Godfrey Owinoh, John Karimi and Donald Mokaya. Most of all I thank Jeff Amusala for his undivided attention, advice and assistance during data analysis.

I thank God for His sustenance and Grace that saw me through the accomplishment of the strenuous task of preparing this thesis.

Lastly, I thank all those who read through drafts of this thesis and provided valuable comments, additional information and suggestions that helped me improve its quality and to all unmentioned people who in their special ways contributed towards accomplishment of this work.

Contents

List of Tables

List of Figures

List of Plates

List of Abbreviations

BMI	Body Mass Index
CBS	Central Bureau of Statistics
CUP	240 millilitres
GM	Grams
KG	Kilogram
MG	Milligram
ML	Millilitres
MUAC	Mid Upper Arm Circumference
NAO	National Audit Office
N.I.P.S.	Northern Ireland Prison Service
OLS	Ordinary Least Squares
Oz	Ounce
TBLS	Tablespoon
TSP	Teaspoon

CHAPTER ONE

Introduction

The hospitality product consists of tangible and intangible elements of food, drink and accommodation together with the service, atmosphere and image that surround and contribute to the product. Public sector catering or welfare catering is a type of catering establishment in hospitality. The establishments under this category include hospitals, universities, schools, prisons, armed forces and meals on wheels. This category of catering is characterized by its non profit making focus, minimizing cost by maximizing efficiency. However, with the introduction of competitive tendering, many public sector operations have been won by contract caterers who have introduced new concepts and commercialism within the public sector (Kinton, *et al.* 2005).

According to Davis, *et al.* (2004), subsidized or welfare food and beverage establishments may be defined as those operations in which making a profit from the catering facility is not the outlet's primary concern. Since the operations are either completely or partially subsidized by a parent body, such establishments' primary obligation is the well-being and care of their customers. Unlike customers frequenting commercial sector operations, these customers often do not have a choice of catering facilities, examples being hospitals and schools. Some non-commercial operations are subsidized by government bodies that dictate an allowance per head, or by parent companies that may have a similar arrangement.

Davis, *et al.* (2004) argues that a distinction can be made between institutional catering and employee catering facilities, for example, in hospitals and schools. An important characteristic of this type of catering is that the market is not only restricted to the residents of the institutions but is in most cases also captive. In addition, institutional catering may be completely subsidized.

According to Kinton, *et al.* (2005), the armed forces catering services include feeding armed services staff in barracks, in the mess and in the field. Much of the work is specialized, especially field cookery. The author is of the view that the forces, like every other section of the public sector, are looking to reduce costs and increase efficiency. They too have been forced to implement market testing and competitive tendering, resulting in contract caterers taking over many service operations. He further alludes that the aim of welfare catering is to minimize cost and cover overheads by achieving maximum efficiency. The standards of cooking should be equally good, though the types of menu may be different.

According to Kinton, *et al.* (2005), hospital catering is classified as welfare catering; its objective is to assist the nursing staff to get the patient well as soon as possible. The same author states further that to do this, it is necessary to provide good quality food, which has been carefully prepared and cooked to retain the maximum nutritional value, and presented to the patient in an appetizing manner. It is recognized that the provision of an adequate diet is just as much a part of the patient's treatment as careful nursing and skilled medical attention. In nearly all hospitals patients are provided with a menu choice.

Prisons work on a very limited budget (Davis, *et al.* 2004). The diet for inmates is based upon fixed weekly quantities of specific named food commodities with a small weekly cash allowance per head for fresh meat and a further separate weekly cash allowance per head for the local purchase of dietary extras of which a proportion must be spent on fresh fruit. The catering services within the prisons is the responsibility of the prison governor with delegated responsibility being given to a catering officer, with much of the actual cooking and service being done by the inmates themselves.

Chabari and Kibosia, (2007) noted the need to address food and catering services as it has an impact on prisoner's health in Kenya. Furthermore, poor nutrition is a major factor in the poor health and causes many diseases among the Kenyan prisoners. Accordingly, it should be noted that the type of food prisoners eat is not bad per se; rather the environment under which it is prepared, the facilities used to prepare it and the manner in which it is prepared make the food less nutritious and hazardous to health. Consequently, Chabari and Kibosia believe that, there is need to overhaul and revamp the prison catering system. This involves the procurement and installation of modern catering facilities including purchase and installation of modern stainless steel plates and dishes for serving the food. The duo further noted that in many prisons, food is prepared in open and unhygienic structures, hence the need for new kitchens to be constructed.

Bosworth, (2004) has argued that concerns about food are often related to how and when meals are distributed. The serving line at meals is a constant reminder of the diners' vulnerability and their powerlessness over the daily routine. Sanitary prescriptions in kitchens and dining rooms may or may not be rigidly enforced, and on hot days in poorly ventilated sweltering areas, the servers' perspiration, mingled with steam from the trays, may drip into the food. In addition, there are prevalent rumors that some inmates "sabotage" food with saliva, faeces, or other matter perpetuating the image of uncleanliness. Although there are few documented cases of foreign substances such as faeces or saliva added to the food during preparation, the rumors contribute to lack of confidence in prison sanitation, especially for prisoners isolated in segregation units to whom food is delivered. While usually delivered in a covered wagon from the central kitchen, food served in this way may not only be vulnerable to hygiene problems but frequently arrive cold.

Another problem is that identified by Beckford and Gilliat, (1998), and it relates to the hour at which meals are served and the amount of time available to eat. Most meal times occur in prison far earlier than is the practice in the free society. Prisoners must, therefore, become accustomed to an entirely new eating schedule that may commence as early as 6am and end by 4pm. Generally, no more than 14 hours may elapse between the evening and breakfast meals. Thus, religious inmates fasting during Ramadhan or Passover sign a waiver form, articulating that they have chosen to go hungry for more than the allowed time period. In most institutions, mealtime is short, usually about a half an hour from entry to exit. If the queues into the dining hall or through the "chow line" are slow, the time for eating is reduced proportionately. Inmates are taken to the dining hall from their cellblocks or assignments in lines, with one line entering when the previous group exits. Although variations occur within and across prison systems, dining generally follow a highly structured regimen.

Additionally, Beckford and Gilliat (1998), stated that prison food can be repetitive despite variation in menus. This occurs in part because of poor preparation resulting in meals in which soggy vegetables and overcooked meat, for example, are indistinguishable from one meal to the next. Some institutions attempt to overcome the problems associated with the provision of food by making cooking facilities available to inmates.

Ekwuruke (2006), stated that "Man is free by nature but his freedom is a consequence of responsibility. In his teachings he implies that an irresponsible man is not free. Hence the philosophy of imprisonment is to make the irresponsible person responsible without violating his dignity as a human being.

There are several areas of primary importance in prison food. These include anything from simple cleanliness problems and rodent infestations, to problems endemic to prisons such as outbreaks of infectious disease (given the presence of so many people in close proximity) and food poisoning. Note that these cases are often linked to other issues, most notably overcrowding. As more people are placed into prison, sanitation becomes an even bigger issue.

Bourn (1997) reported that Prison caterers do well in difficult conditions whereas, the main problems which reduce quality ratings are the inadequacy of storage arrangements, food cooked too far in advance, delivery times, lack of wastage monitoring, and limited information on food quality. In addition, he noted that most prisoners received their last meal of the day at around 4.30pm while variations in the quality of produce supplied ranged from two prisons with consistently high quality produce to one which produced a consistently low quality.

The Prisons Act Cap 90 of the Laws of Kenya stipulates the mode and sequence of events at the prisons and particularly the administration of food to prisoners, administration of the penal diet of prison officers and the scale of diets for all prisoners respectively. The Prisons Act Cap 90 is the reference point in this study since it is the creator of the specific food menu items and frequency of consumption for the prisoners. Specifically, sections 49, 51 and 118 of the Prisons Act Cap 90 set out the administration of food to prisoners, administration of the penal diet by prison officers and the scale of diet for all prisoners respectively. The Prisons Act Cap 90 also outlines the specific food menu items and frequency of consumption for prisoners.

Statement of the Problem

The quality of catering in Kenyan prisons is an issue of much concern to the government and the entire society. The type of food served to prisoners may result in an increase in diseases and poor health, hardening the behaviour of prisoners, leading to grievances in prisons, protests and strikes. In spite of this alarming situation, there has been little effort made to improve prison catering which might have otherwise helped in the rehabilitation of prisoners in Kenya. Accordingly, if the conditions and standards of catering in Kenyan prisons are not addressed, opportunities for reforming as well as re-integrating prisoners into the mainstream society might be in jeopardy, hence the need for this study.

According to Korane (2000), Kenyan prisons are in very poor conditions in all the provinces and that all facilities are pathetic. These harsh conditions end up hardening criminals rather than rehabilitating them. In these conditions, infectious diseases such as diarrhoea, typhoid, tuberculosis and HIV & AIDS spread easily (*East Africa Standard*, 20th September 2000). The poor conditions might result in loss of dignity and low self esteem of prisoners hence making it hard for them to reform.

According to a report by Amnesty International (2000), conditions in many Kenyan prisons are not only cruel but amount to inhuman and degrading treatment. Hundreds of prisoners die each year, some as a result of torture by prison officers, the majority from infectious diseases resulting from severe overcrowding, unsanitary conditions, and shortages of food, clean water, clothing, blankets and inadequate medical care. A statement about the conditions in one police cell by Wanjohi (1997) graphically depicts the inhuman conditions in prisons, "There is a bucket provided in each cell at Isiolo Police Station to serve as a toilet. At times the floor is flooded with urine and faeces. Those held have to take their meals in this foul environment. The cells in Isiolo Prison stink and the floors often overflow with human waste."

Furthermore, the quality and the quantity of food served in prisons leaves much to be desired (Wanjohi, 1997). In Langata Prison, for instance, children incarcerated with their mothers get the same diet as their mothers, and this usually "half-cooked and sugarless porridge made from rotten flour." According to Wanjohi, (1997) in some prisons such as Eldoret, the quantity of food is so inadequate that inmates resort to buying food from the prison's catering staff. The catering staff reportedly steal the food to sell it back to the inmates or take it to their homes. Consequently, prisoners who cannot afford to buy food literally starve or resort to dishonorable means of survival. A former Kenyan prisoner called Ngengi stated that, "Some prisoners collected fallen *ugali* from the ground due to hunger". He further claimed to have seen grown men cry due to hunger.

In protest against hunger and general inhuman conditions, prisoners have occasionally been reported to stage riots. The *Daily Nation* of June 12, 2000, for instance, reported that over 200 inmates at Rumuruti Prison in Rift Valley Province, rioted over a food shortage. One prisoner died and scores were injured after prison officers intervened to end the riot. In another earlier incident reported in the *Daily Nation* of November 19, 1999, prisoners complained that food rations were halved to 250 grams per day and three quarters of a pint of porridge in Kodiaga Prison, Nyanza Province, in order to cut prison costs.

According to Bosworth (2004), there is the use of food, or the withdrawal of food, as a form of punishment. Thus, in some cases a prison might withhold food from inmates that do not conform to the rules. There is also the issue of special diets. Bosworth (2004), continued to say that often inmates have special dietary needs, either for health or religious reasons. Examples here include diabetics and Muslims who require special food and non pork foods respectively. Furthermore, food services do not comply with all applicable standards. For example, the amount of time between dinner and breakfast is supposed to be thirteen hours, but given the constraints of the prison schedule, this much time is not always given.

Several cases of cholera deaths have been reported by Kenyan Health authorities since 2008 and new cases continue to be reported. The Daily Nation Newspapers dated 23-03-2009 and 24-03-2009 reported that fifteen inmates in Nakuru GK Prison were admitted to hospital and two inmates died after they contracted the disease. Standard Newspaper dated 24-03-2009 reported subsequent cases at the Kakamega Prison where one inmate had died while eight others were hospitalized. The reports further claimed that the disease may have been brought by some inmates transferred from Naivasha Prison. The health officials blamed the spread of the disease from the prisons on the "colonial nature" of the water storage facilities that exist in those detention facilities and warned that the public health authorities would order a total overhaul of the tanks. Cholera is a water borne disease and is normally transmitted through drinking of contaminated water, living under unsanitary conditions, eating food that was not well-cooked and not washing hands after visiting the toilet. If not treated, death can occur from 12-18 hours.

Edwards, *et al*. (2001), researched on "The nutritional content of male prisoners' diet in the UK". Godderis (2006), researched on "The Symbolic Power of Food in Prison" while Smith (2002), researched on "Punishment and pleasure of women, food and the imprisoned body". However, there seem to be no research done on quality of catering in prisons and hence no documents available for reference. Accordingly, the researcher attempts to fill the existing knowledge gap.

Purpose of the Study

The purpose of this study was to investigate factors affecting the quality of catering offered in prisons, firstly, in terms of the type of food given to prisoners, secondly, the way food was prepared and thirdly, how the food was served. The study also compared the prisoner's diet as per the Prisons Act Cap. 90 with the actual food they received. The study sought to make recommendations to Kenya Prison Service Department regarding the management of quality of catering in prisons and how the discipline of catering can be used in rehabilitating prisoners in order to promote their opportunities for social reintegration and eventually community protection. It is expected that if prisoners reform, they become peace loving citizens and desist from crime which eventually culminates in a safe environment.

Research Objectives

General Objective.
The main objective of this study was to examine and provide an understanding of the factors that affect the quality of catering in Kenyan prisons.

The Specific Objectives
1. To investigate the extent to which the type of food served to prisoners affects the quality of catering in Kenyan prisons.
2. To find out the extent to which food preparation affects the quality of catering in Kenyan prisons.
3. To establish how food service affects the quality of catering in Kenyan prisons.
4. To determine the extent to which the actual food served to prisoners differs from the menu items contained in the Prisons Act Cap 90

Research Questions
The study sought to answer the following research questions:
1. To what extent does the type of food served to prisoners affect the quality of catering in Kenyan prisons?
2. To what extent does food preparation affect the quality of catering in Kenyan prisons?
3. How does food service affect the quality of catering in Kenyan prisons?
4. To what extent does the actual food served to prisoners differ from the menu items contained in the Prisons Act, Cap 90?

Hypotheses
H_1: Type of food served to prisoners affects the quality of catering in prisons.

H_2: Food preparation in prison affects the quality of catering.

H_3: Food service in prison affects the quality of catering.

H_4: Actual food served to prisoners differs from menu items contained in the Prisons Act Cap 90.

Assumptions of the Study

The following were the assumptions on the study;

(a) That the researcher accessed all catering areas necessary for the study

(b) That prisoners and warders gave true and honest information.

(c) That prison warders did not unduly influence the opinions of inmates

(d) That prisoners and prison warders interviewed had adequate knowledge to comment on the issues regarding catering in prisons and that they understood all the questions asked.

Rationale of the Study

The study on the factors affecting the quality of catering in prisons was important because it provided information which shed light on the dynamics of catering in captive markets. Some of the factors of interest included the type of food served in prisons, the methods of food production used and the way food was served in prisons. Good catering services within the prison can immensely contribute to higher productivity from the prisoners in terms of provision of labour to the government and society and the general behavioral change of the prisoners. In addition quality catering can result in good health of prisoners on their release hence result in productive citizens on their re-entry to society. Some of the strikes and diseases faced in prisons could be due to shortages in food resulting from the limited resources allocated to prison food by the government.

The findings of the study will go along way in helping to uncover the causes of poor catering services in prisons and therefore make the understanding of it. The results of this study may be used as a reflection of what is happening in prisons and thus offer advice on how to reduce its effects.

Significance of the Study

The results of the study are expected to address the real situation about the quality of catering in Kenyan prisons. The study was significant in mapping out a way forward to improving the factors that affect the quality of catering in prisons in terms of type of food, food preparation and service. In addition, the study findings are expected to benefit the government of Kenya which is in the process of reforming the Prisons Department. Specifically the study has given recommendations regarding the right food preparation and service methods that can be adopted as well as hygiene measures that should be put into place or improved where they exist. In general, the study was to contribute to the improvement of prisoners' welfare in Kenya through the recommendations made to the government and other relevant stakeholders towards rehabilitation and ways of using catering services in prison to facilitate training of prisoners for their re-entry into societal life stream. Finally, other researchers and scholars in this area might borrow a leaf from this study which will have also extended the scope of knowledge.

Very little research has been done in catering in prisons which was evidenced by lack of adequate literature from libraries hence the findings of this study are an eye opener to other areas of catering in prisons.

Scope of the Study

The scope of factors affecting quality of catering for the purposes of this study included the type of food served to prisoners, the methods used in the preparation of food in prisons and the way food was served in prisons. The study was limited to catering practices in the five prisons which enabled the researcher to focus the study on a specific area. The study focused on ordinary and convicted prisoners serving short and long sentences. The study was conducted for a period of seven months. In addition, the study compared the menu items stipulated in the Prisons Act Cap 90 against the actual food served to prisoners. The study did not include other aspects that could contribute to the quality of catering such as the quality of food supplied to prisons, the suppliers of food items, the storage of food and the amount of funds allocated by the government for catering.

Challenges Faced in the Study

The following challenges were faced by the researcher in the study:

1. Inability by the researcher to access the prisons for surprise visits to the catering areas for observations which may have omitted some information that may have been vital for the study. The prisons were accessible only after 9am hence observation of breakfast was impossible.

2. Prison warders attempted to influence the prisoners responses by warning them not to let out prison secrets. However, most of the prisoners defied the threats after the researcher assured them of confidentiality and anonymity of the information given on questionnaires

3. There was inadequate literature on previous publications as there was no evidence of any research carried out in relation to catering services in Kenyan prisons. However collection of data from different sources addressed this aspect.

4. The prison warders interviewed feared being victimized if they divulged information hence they may have withheld vital information for this study.

5. Inability to participate in randomly selecting the prisoners to interview for security reasons hence the warders assisted

Theoretical Framework of the Study

A theoretical framework is a collection of interrelated concepts, like a theory but not necessarily so well worked-out. A theoretical framework guides' research, determining what things the researcher will measure, and what statistical relationships will be looked for.

Reinforcement Theory

This study was based on the reinforcement theory put forth by B.F. Skinner (1974). The reinforcement theory suggests that a given behaviour is a function of the consequences of earlier behaviour. Thus, it is argued, all behaviour is determined to some extent by the rewards or punishments obtained from previous behaviour, which has the effect of reinforcing current actions. In this sense all behaviour is caused by external sources, since we can have little control over the consequences of our actions.

In light of the above stipulation, then it can be argued that prisoners are in prison as a consequence of their past behaviour (crimes or other illegal activities) and that their sentences in prison are meant to reform them (instill positive behaviour) into law abiding citizens. However, while in prison, the prisoners are subjected to poor feeding which include poor quality and quantity of food, penal diets and unhygienic conditions. All this happens despite the fact that prisoners engage in productive activities while in prison that generate income to the Prisons Service Department. As a consequence of poor feeding in prison in Kenya, prisoners turn to such desperate acts such as homosexuality to access a good meal. Again, their integrity as human beings' is compromised by the poor meals fed to them and some are easily transformed into more hardcore criminals. Clearly then, the reform agenda of the Prisons Service Department may not be realized.

This study argues that if prisoners were fed on a decent meal, under good hygienic conditions, then this would be very instrumental in building their self esteem and instilling good behaviour into the prisoners and thus the realization of the reform agenda by Prisons Service Department. The prisoners would feel appreciated and put more effort into their various assignments in prison and this would in turn help them integrate well in society upon release. Furthermore, if catering in prisons could be used to train prisoners in catering or any other discipline and thereafter issue certificates upon completing, it would lead to capacity building and may increase chances of them being employed after imprisonment which could reinforce positive behaviour and make it possible to realize reforms.

Supporters of reinforcement theory such as Jablonsky and De Vries, (1972) offer some important guidelines to those intending to use it as a motivating tool in the work place. Typical suggestions include; positively reinforce desired behaviour and avoid using punishment as principle means of achieving desired performance. The use of penal code as a way of correcting prisoners should be repealed since it may not necessarily achieve the intended goal/ purpose.

Further suggestions include applying positive reinforcement regularly. Prisoners should be appreciated for work they do while serving their sentences through being fed well to encourage their participation in reform activities undertaken by the Prisons Service Department. Other suggestions by proponents of this theory include ignoring undesired behaviour as much as possible and providing reinforcement as soon as possible after the response. It further suggests that assessing positive and negative factors in the individuals' environment and specifying desired behaviour/performance in quantifiable terms

The underlying assumption behind this approach is that people are there to be controlled and that management's task is to provide the "right" conditions to encourage high performance. This assumption holds true for the Kenyan Prisons Service Department situation and hence its applicability.

Conceptual Framework of the Study

Prisoners, just like other customers of captive markets have their expectations of the quality of catering. The conceptual framework for the study is as shown in figure 1.1. models the relationship between the type of food, food preparation and service and the quality of catering in prisons. The Independent variables in this study were defined in three broad categories, which comprised type of food served to prisoners, food preparation and food service.

According to the model, the type of food was determined by the aesthetic value of food, the nutritive value of food and the purpose of food. Food preparation was determined by food preparation methods, cooking equipment, cooking persons, the hygiene of the food preparation area, time of preparation and ingredients used. Food service was determined by the temperature of food, service persons, equipment used for serving, methods of service, time of serving food, place of service, quantity of food served and hygiene of food service area.

The antecedent variable was the Prisons Act Cap 90 that stipulates the menu items to be consumed by prisoners and other sections that lay out rules and guidance for the management of prison food. The Prisons Act has a direct influence on the independent variables which eventually influence the dependent variable. The dependent variable was the quality of catering which was directly influenced by the independent variables.

According to the model, the quality of food was affected by the type of food, the preparation of food and the service of food. All these factors are indirectly affected by the Prisons Act Cap 90 which contains details on the management of food in Kenyan Prisons.

Figure 1.1 The Conceptual Framework

Model showing the relationship of the key variables of quality of catering in Kenyan prisons

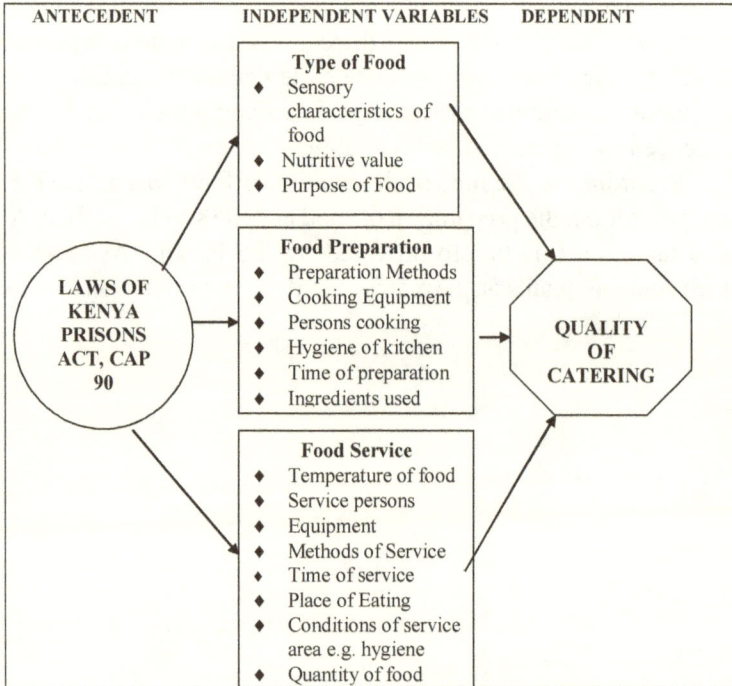

ANTECEDENT	INDEPENDENT VARIABLES	DEPENDENT

Type of Food
- Sensory characteristics of food
- Nutritive value
- Purpose of Food

Food Preparation
- Preparation Methods
- Cooking Equipment
- Persons cooking
- Hygiene of kitchen
- Time of preparation
- Ingredients used

LAWS OF KENYA PRISONS ACT, CAP 90

QUALITY OF CATERING

Food Service
- Temperature of food
- Service persons
- Equipment
- Methods of Service
- Time of service
- Place of Eating
- Conditions of service area e.g. hygiene
- Quantity of food

Author's own Compilation, (2008)

The factors in the independent variables combine and impact on the quality of catering in Prison to arrive at the decision as to whether the quality of catering is good or poor. The outcome of the unfavorable quality of catering may result in difficulty in rehabilitating prisoners and re-integrating them into society.

CHAPTER TWO

Literature Review

Overview

This chapter reviewed literature relevant to the research problem under four broad sections; quality of catering which was the dependent variable in this study; type of prison food in some parts of the world under which there are seven subsections dealing with prison menus, nutritional requirements of different people, retaining nutrient content of foods, assessing nutrition of adults, special meals in prison, food as punishment in prisons and the cultural significance of food; food preparation in prisons; and lastly, food service in Prisons with two subsections dealing in the number and timing of meals and recommended servings. Finally, the Kenyan recommended prison food menu as stipulated in the Prisons Act, CAP 90 is presented.

Quality of Catering

According to Scanlon, (2007) the term "quality" is difficult to define in relation to hospitality operations but easy to recognize. Quality is a perception of how good or bad a product is based on an individual's points of reference. He further states that training is an important factor in implementation of a quality-service program hence training for all employees is critical to maintaining a standard of quality service. However he alludes that the first step in establishing quality is to identify the level of quality to be produced. An overall level of quality for products and services should be determined for the particular target markets that a catering business services.

According to New Zealand Qualifications Authority, (2009) which is a standard setting body in accreditation and moderation of standards in that country, there are three elements and performance criteria used to supervise and monitor the quality of food production, foodservice and the catering staff in a food service catering operation.

Firstly, is the quality of food production whereby the performance criteria ranges from procedure that include but not limited to recipes and menus, cooking methods, receiving and storage of goods. Further food preparation is monitored to ensure all customers' dietary requirements are met in accordance with establishment and dietary requirements. Hence food production quality includes but not limited to taste, texture, quantity, fitness for purpose, appearance and wastage. Secondly, is food service which the performance criteria includes factors but not limited to establishment culture, sequence of service, standards for service and safe food handling. The quality standards of food service include but are not limited to presentation of food, service of food, temperature of food, transportation and wastage of food during service.

Lastly, in supervising and monitoring the quality of food, the catering staff in the food service catering operation in terms of the staffing numbers, rosters, experience and the integration of new staff into the existing team in terms of induction and on-going team development.

The SERVQUAL Model

The SERVQUAL model (Figure 2.1) can be operationalised by both qualitative and quantitative research. The model measures tangible and intangible service elements (Parasuraman, Zeithaml and Berry, 1990). It defines quality as the differences between customers' expectations and perceptions of service delivery. The model therefore, investigates discrepancies or gaps in the consumer – supply to highlight target areas where quality may be improved. Specifically, the model shows the relationship between the external gap 5 and the internal gaps 1-4. Gap 5 depends on the size and direction of the four gaps. If gaps 1-4 are reduced, the service quality can be improved, hence gap 5 can also be reduced.

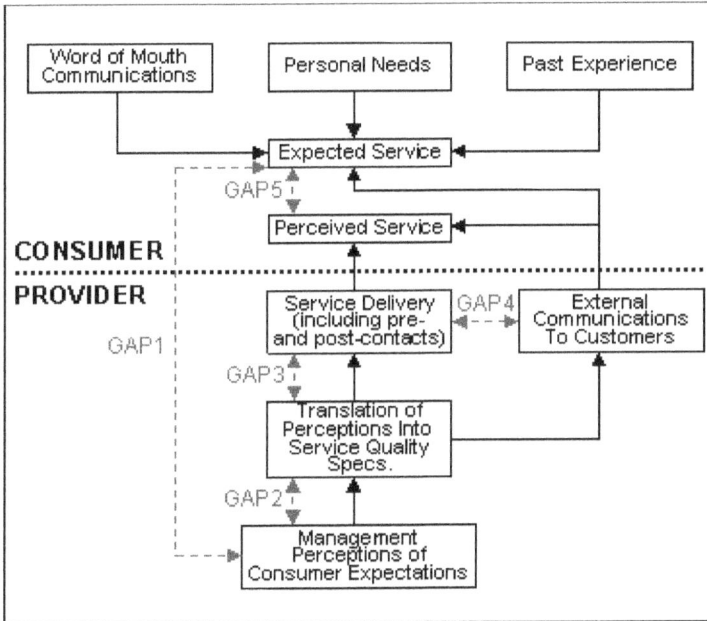

Source: Parasuraman, et al,(1990)

Figure 2.1: The SERVQUAL Model

The SERVQUAL instrument has been proposed as an instrument for the measurement of perceived service quality within a wide range of service categories. However, there has been no catering related replication of the initial SERVQUAL work nor any refinement of the instrument based on its application to catering.

The upper part of the model includes phenomena tied to the consumer, while the lower part shows phenomena tied to the supplier of services. The expected service is the function of earlier experiences of the consumer, their personal needs and oral communication. Communication with the market also influences the expected service. Experienced service, here called perceived service, is the result of a series of internal decisions and activities. The management's perception of the consumer's expectations is the guiding principle when deciding on the specifications of the quality of service that the company should follow in providing service. If there are differences or discrepancies in the expectations or perceptions between people involved in providing and consuming services, a "service quality gap" can occur, as shown in Fig 1. Since there is a direct connection between the quality of service and the satisfaction of clients in hotel industry, it is important for the company to spot a gap in the quality of service.

The first possible gap is management perceptions of consumer expectations. It is the result of the management's lack of full understanding about how consumers formulate their expectations on the basis of a number of sources including advertising, past experience, personal needs and communication with friends. This gap can lead to other gaps in the process of service quality and is, among other things, caused by: incorrect information in market researches and demand analysis; incorrect interpretations of information regarding expectations; lack of information about any feedback between the company and the consumers directed to the management; and too many organizational layers that hinder or modify parts of information in their upward movement from those involved in contact with the consumers. This gap can be closed by learning what customers expect through the use of market research, forecasting better communication and reducing the number of levels of management that distance the customer. Other strategies for closing this gap include complaint analysis and customer panels; increasing direct interactions between managers and customers; improving upward communications; and acting on information and insights.

The second possible gap is wrong service quality standards. It is the result of management's inability to formulate target levels of service quality to meet perceptions of customers' expectations and translates these into workable specifications. This gap may result from a lack of management commitment to service quality or a perception of the unfeasibility of meeting customers' expectations. It emanates from mistakes in planning or insufficient planning procedures; bad management planning; lack of clearly set goals in the organization; and insufficient support of the top management to service quality planning. The management can be right in evaluating the client's expectations and develop business methods to satisfy these expectations, without the employees being correct in providing service. However, setting goals and standardizing service delivery tasks can close this gap.

The third possible gap is service performance. In this gap, the actual delivery of service does not meet the specifications set by management. It arises from lack of teamwork, poor employee selection, inadequate training and inappropriate job design.

The fourth possible gap is the communication gap arising when promises do not match delivery of service. This gap results from discrepancy between service delivery and external communications in the form of exaggerated promises and lack of information provided to contact personnel. The reasons are: the planning of communication with the market is not integrated with the services; lack or insufficient coordination between traditional marketing and procedures; organizational performance not in keeping with the specifications, while the policy of communication with the market abides by the given specifications; and tendency to exaggerate in accordance with exaggerated promises.

The fifth gap is the difference between what the customers expected to receive from the service and what the service provider believes they actually gave.

Should any of the mentioned gaps arise; the "service gap" will also appear because the real service will not satisfy the client's expectations. Hotel companies try to detect the "service gap" with survey questionnaires.

Type of Prison Food in Some Parts of the World

Experiences of American, Britain, parts of Africa and other parts of the world have been reviewed in this sub-section. The experiences were accessible to the researcher.

American Experience

According to Bosworth, (2004) traditionally, food was used in prisons as a means of reward and punishment. In the nineteenth century, for example, incoming prisoners were often served bread and water until they had earned the right for such luxuries as meat or cheese. In the Eastern penitentiary in Philadelphia, breakfast was sparse and monotonous, consisting of coffee, cocoa or green tea, and a mix of bread and Indian mush. The primary meal at midday consisted of substantial portions of boiled pork or beef, soup, potatoes or rice, sauerkraut, and tea. Indian mush and tea constituted the evening meal.

Bosworth (2004) states further that in recent decades, the science of nutrition has remained crucial to the provision of food in most prisons. Usually, diets are carefully planned and standardized. Some facilities post the weekly menu, including nutritional analyses of each meal listing caloric, fat, cholesterol and sodium content of each prepared item. In addition, all federal prisons are meant to have a salad bar and offer a 'heart healthy' version of the main meal. Fried and baked chicken, for example, or french fries and baked potatoes may be served at the same meal.

State prison systems, however, vary dramatically, in part because contracting food services out to the private sector is becoming increasingly common (Pens 2001). However, because of both formal and informal pressures, such as prison reform efforts, prisoner litigation challenges conditions, and the nation wide influence of the American Correctional Association in providing minimal standards before individual prisons receive accreditation, prison food has improved dramatically.

According to Greenwood, (2008) the United States Supreme Court consistently ruled that prisoners have the right to an adequate and varied diet, including the right to tailor meals to religious prescriptions and medical needs. However, Greenwood, (2008) continues to state that the provision of food in prison often remains a sore point for inmates. Problems include food and preparation quality, portion sizes, and the temperature at which it is served. Nutraloaf (sometimes called Nutri-loaf, sometimes just "the loaf") is served in state prisons around the country. It's not part of the regular menu but is prescribed for inmates who have misbehaved in various ways—usually by proving untrustworthy with their utensils. The loaf provides a full day's nutrients, and its finger food, meaning that no cutlery is necessary.

British Experience

According to N.I.P.S, (2008) in Northern Ireland, almost every prisoner is faced with the problem of cockroach infestation throughout the prison. Many of them find cockroaches in their food. In the kitchen area no cockroaches are seen and the food-preparation area is clean. However, orderlies in the food preparation area joked about 'rat fights' and the preponderance of 'traditional Belfast roaches'.

N.I.P.S., (2008) state that prison catering departments are required, under the Northern Ireland Prison and Young Offenders Rules 1995 to.... *'provide every prisoner with sufficient food which is wholesome, nutritious, palatable, adequately presented and well prepared and which takes into account age, health, and work and, as far as practicable, religious or cultural requirement'* (Rule 82). The main objective of every Prison Service catering team is: *'to provide a varied and healthy menu which takes account of prisoner's preferences whilst maintaining compliance with all relevant food safety legislation'*.

African Experience

In Zimbabwe, prisoners are forced to go without food as inflation devoured prisons' food budget. Harare, 12 June 2006 (IRIN) reported that Zimbabwe's economic crisis is reaching into prisons cells, often forcing inmates to go without food for days, the findings of two parliamentary committees revealed. Shortage of food and a lack of water, sanitation and health services were some of the problems in police cells and prisons across the country. According to the Highlands Police Station on the eastern outskirts of the capital, Harare, "The shortage of food was said to have been exacerbated by the shortage of maize. Suspects were said to have gone for two days without food and some were relying on food brought by relatives."

Lausanne, (2008) reported that the Rwandan government banned persons from bringing food for prisoners. Harerimana (2008) was quoted at the state radio saying that the government considered that the food intake served in the prisons was sufficient. According to Lausanne (2008), the back and forth movement of people bringing food to prisoners prevents people from engaging in other productive activities.

Last (2006) stated that in Nigeria, prison food is basic and the ration small, usually a bowl of beans in the morning and cassava in the afternoon and evening. Some rely on their families to bring food to the prison. Former inmates say money can buy better conditions - the guards taking their cut. Accordingly, prison officials, police, and security forces often denied inmates food and medical treatment as a form of punishment or to extort money from them. Last (2006) said that prison reform groups say that there have been at least five prison riots.

Many prisons in Nigeria have no toilet facilities, and cells lack water. Medical facilities are severely limited; food, which represented 80 percent of annual prison expenditures, was inadequate, despite a prison agricultural program designed to produce local foodstuffs for the commercial market. Malnutrition and disease were therefore rampant. In May 1987 at Benin Prison, armed police killed twenty-four inmates rioting over food supplies. (http://www.country-data.com/cgi_bin/query/r-9483.html)

Ekwuruke, (2005) stated that Nigerian prisons today had limitations glaringly manifesting themselves such as inadequate feeding and the prisoners are offered the poorest quality of food, which is also unbalanced with good quantity. Ekwuruke, (2005) goes further to state that even the little the prisoners are offered is eaten in filthy and dirty cells, unhealthy for food consumption. Accommodation/ Overcrowding: This is the most irritating problem in most Nigerian prisons. To substantiate this assertion, a cell at Ikoyi Lagos Prisons of 500 inmates is used by more than 2000 inmates. Still, in some cells, bedrooms, toilets, dinning halls and living rooms are combined together.

Labo, (2006) says that "The two main problems in Nigerian prisons are congestion and lack of food." He continues to explain that the daily ration generally consists of a bowl of beans in the morning then cassava in the afternoon and evening. Prisons have a budget of 150 Naira (US $1.15) per prisoner per day. But this small amount does not necessarily get to all prisoners. Conditions favour disease, lack of food moreover aggravates already poor hygiene conditions. Further, Labo, (2006) said that malnutrition makes prisoners highly vulnerable to infectious diseases such as tuberculosis or skin diseases caused by lack of hygiene.

Other Experiences

Phinney, (2004) stated that prison food in Iraq is rotten food crawling with bugs, traces of rats and dirt. Rancid meats and spoiled food result in diarrhea and food poisoning. He claims that detainees at the Abu Ghraib prisoners near Baghdad were regularly given to eat by a private contractor in late 2003 and early 2004. Foul as the food was, there never was enough when the food did arrive; it was often late and frequently contaminated.

According to Amnesty International, (2005) cell-bound prisoners do not get sufficient food or medicines and conditions inside the prison have deteriorated so seriously that prisoners face imminent risk of starvation. Provision of food by the authorities was reduced from a cup of rice daily in December 2004 to one or two bread rolls a day, and since the end of February 2005 provision of any prison food has been sporadic, with prisoners reportedly going for up to six days at a time without any food.

The same Amnesty International report stated that prisoners and detainees are dependent on food handed to prison guards by families. This means that foreign nationals and dozens of Equatorial Guinean political detainees arrested on the mainland particularly risk starvation because they do not have families in the country to support them. Bowen Stephen notes: 'Such near starvation, lack of medical attention and appalling prison conditions are nothing short of a slow, lingering death sentence for these prisoners. 'The authorities must provide food and medicine and grant access to international monitors.

Prison Menus

This sub-section reviews menu items served in some prisons in the world.

Trenton Prison meals served are similar to those consumed by many average American families (Bosworth, 2004). In addition to that, according to Donovan, (1982) prison food is as good and nutritious as those that many American families eat. According to Donovan, (1982) for inmates in the state's correctional facilities, a typical breakfast menu consists of cereal, toast, jam, jelly, doughnuts, coffee and fruit. Lunch may be spaghetti with meatballs, salad with dressing, bread or rolls, brownies and milk. And the dinner menu may show meat loaf with mushroom gravy, Spanish rice, buttered collard greens, bread and butter, jelly and milk.

The following is a typical menu from Long Lartin prison, a high security dispersal prison in Worcestershire, Britain. It was described by the National Audit Office as 'satisfactory' (Flynn, et al. 1998).

Table 2.1 Prison menus, Worcestershire, 2008

Breakfast	boiled egg, toast, marmalade, or cereals, toast, marmalade, or Porridge, toast
Lunch	macaroni cheese, or quiche, or sausage rolls (with potato/rice and bread)
Tea	vegetable stir fry, or roast pork and gravy, or braised liver and onions, or French bread pizza.

Source: *Flynn, et al (1998)*

Wyke, (2007) noted that in Italian prisons harvested fruit (including grapes, peaches, cherries, strawberries and figs) and vegetables (including tomatoes, courgettes, aubergines,) are incorporated into the prison menus. The prisoners even get 250ml of wine per day in a plastic bottle. With all this fresh organic produce prisoners eat better than most citizens.

In general "the quality and quantity of food is of an excellent standard – the diets are varied and healthy. The menu is based on typical Italian cooking, including pasta and minestrone and other Mediterranean specialties." He continued to state that "the coffee is superb in prison prepared with extreme care and attention, and sweets and pastries made with as much imagination as possible in the environment and also "in prison you're never short of time to think and the creative genius of Italians is expressed in the most unexpected ways" (Wyke 2007)

In Uganda, prisoners eat *posho*, a maize-based starch food, bean soup, and unboiled water. The bean soup is only the liquid cooked with beans, not the beans themselves. Kyomya M. a medical superintendent of the main hospital at Luzira Prison situated in Murchison Bay, is of the opinion that the food was enough for energy but grossly inadequate for vitamins and minerals (Glenna 2008).

In Zimbabwe, according to Chibvuri, (1997) Breakfast consists of tea and bread. Lunch is a cup of boiled rice and a leafy, green vegetable boiled to a stage of no nutritional value. Supper is the same as lunch, with the exception that four times a week boiled minced beef or pork is substituted for the vegetable. Approximately

20 grams of mince is supplied and often it is rotten. It is not uncommon for prisoners to be charged with bestiality with the pigs that are bred for consumption in this prison. Sometimes the vegetable they are given is of a variety not fit for human consumption and occasionally it is contaminated with bugs and grass from the fields in which it is cultivated. Frequently rat faeces are cooked with their rice, and the medical milk ration is normally undrinkable due to it being sour or curdled.

In India, Lunch and dinner typically include piping hot rice, two vegetables and a spicy lentil dish called *sambar* and buttermilk. A dessert is added on festival days and national holidays like Independence Day, and also once a week. (http://www.ananova.com/news/story/sm2384948.html)

Kenya Prisons Act Cap 90

Prisons Act is an Act of Parliament to consolidate and amend the law relating to prisons. It is a set of promulgated rules that mate out on the food menu, ordinary diet, scale diet and penal diet. The Act is paramount as it is the source of the various case studies enumerated in this study.

First Schedule

The Laws of Kenya, Prisons Act Cap 90, under the "first schedule," outlines the food diet for prisoners and children respectively as shown on table 2.2. It states that the Ministry of Home Affairs may make rules providing for the provision of a suitable diet and dietary scales, including punishment diet for prisoners and prescribing the conditions under which such diet and scale may be varied. Details of the prisoner's diet are as show on table 2.2.

Table 2.2 Prisoners Diet (Monday to Sunday), 2008.

Diet	On each 4 days a week	On each 3 days a week
a) Carbohydrates/Vegetables Protein	Grams	Grams
Maize or other cereals	570	570
Beans	225	-
Soya flour	20	-
Green grams (*Ndengu*)	-	230
b) Animal Protein		
Fresh Meat	-	200
Dried skimmed milk	-	500 ml
Sugar	20	20
Salt	15	15
c) Fats		
Fortified vegetable oil or		
Fortified vegetable ghee	16	16
d) Fresh vegetables and fruit		
Green leafy vegetables	120	-
Carrots	-	90
Irish potatoes or sweet potatoes	30	115
Spring onions	30	30
Capsicum	30	30
Tomatoes	-	30

Source: Laws of Kenya, *Prisons Act Cap 90*, Section 74, First Schedule, 2008.
Prisoners & Borstal inmates under escort diet

	Grams
Biscuits	125
Tinned beans	120

Commenced on 1963-02-01.

Sensory Characteristics of Food

According to Sethi, (2008) sensory characteristics of food can be identified by use of senses such as appearance, smell, feel and sound of food. It is common that if food does not look good when served, it will be rejected even if it tastes good. So the appearance of food is important in acceptability which is largely contributed by the colour and texture of foods selected and their presentation to customers.

Sethi (2008) argues that food gets its colour in many different ways including from natural plant and animal pigments; from the effect of heat, chemical reactions, oxidation and synthetic colourants. Colour in foods attract people because of the many different colours they provide in their natural, cooked or processed forms. Fruits and vegetables contain different kinds of pigments which when combined diligently impart the aesthetic qualities of foods. Sethi, (2008) continues to note that depending on the composition of food, heat can affect its colour, flavour, texture and acceptability e.g. when a slice of bread is toasted, it turns brown. Once the appearance of food is good i.e. the eyes are satisfied with the quality of food, the sensory organs of the nose and mouth take over.

According to Sethi (2008), flavour relates to the combined sensation of smell, aroma, taste and the feel of the food in the mouth. Flavour acceptance or rejection, however, is influenced by people's cultural, regional and religious backgrounds. For instance, a person from western, far eastern or Muslim countries would relish the delicate flavour of beef, as against an Indian who would consider the smell unacceptable simply because the two have different eating habits and experiences with food. The age old proverb *"one mans food is another mans poison"* is so apt when dealing with food acceptance. These differences have given rise to specialty menus such as Chinese, continental, vegetarian and so on to suit the tastes and values of different people and account for regional and cultural preferences.

According to Sethi (2008), the role smell plays in food acceptability is clear from the fact that very often odours put people off a food even without their tasting it. Sethi, (2008) states that odours can be described as pungent, minty, putrid, and so on. Pleasant odours generally result from subtle combinations which are delicate and not strong. Mouthfeel is the next component of flavour. Depending on how the food feels in the mouth, it may be rejected if it contains too many chillies or spices which irritate the membranes of the mouth. If the food is too hot in terms of temperature, it causes blisters or pain. Again, the most favourite foods can be rejected if they are too slippery, sticky or hard to bite into. After the odour is accepted, the next sensory characteristics needed for acceptability is taste, that is, the reaction of the taste buds to the food, determining whether it is sweet, sour, salty or bitter. Acceptability of food therefore depends on how well they harmonize to make the net sensation pleasurable.

Sethi (2008) alludes that texture of food can be determined both by perception and mouthfeel. It varies from food to food and in the same food too when different methods of cooking are used. Texture also depends on structural composition of food which can be described as rough, smooth, grainy, coarse, fine, crisp, viscous, spongy and heavy. People accept or reject foods which do not agree with their own mental images regarding shape, size, viscosity or sheen. For example, rice which is overcooked and therefore sticky instead of grainy will not be accepted if customers have a choice.

Nutritional Requirements for a Balanced Diet
Jones, (1988) stated that most foods are a mixture of the different nutrients needed for a well-balanced diet. These nutrients are as follows:

i.   Proteins: An average diet requires about 65grams of protein a day; these are broken down during digestion into amino acids, eight of which are essential to adults' life. Generally speaking, meat, cheese, eggs and fish are higher value protein foods and vegetables are low value foods.

ii. Fats: These basically provide the body with energy, and yield more energy for a given weight than any other nutrient. Some 30-35% of calorie needs for individuals should be derived from this source.

iii. Carbohydrates: These also provide energy, in the form of starch and sugars. To some extent such foods have the function of providing bulk in the diet which assists in increasing bowel movements.

iv. Minerals: These have three functions: bone formation; as dissolved salts in the body fluids to maintain acidity or alkalinity; and as constituents of soft tissues to enable them to carry out their particular function.

v.   Vitamins: These are present in small quantities in food and are needed to prevent specific deficiency diseases.

However, depending upon their age and health, different people have specific dietary requirements.

Table 2.3 Recommended intake of some typical nutrients

	Protein (g)	Thiamin (mg)	Vitamin A (ug)	Iron (mg)
Babies	20-30	0.3-0.5	400	6-7
Infants	35-45	0.6-0.8	300	8-10
Teenage boys	70-75	1.1-1.2	730	14-15
Teenage girls	58	0.9	730	14-15
Adult men – sedentary	65-70	1.0-1.1	750	10
-moderately active	70-75	1.2	750	10
- very active	90	1.4	750	10
Adult women – sedentary and moderately active	55	0.9	750	12
- very active	63	1.0	750	12
Pregnant Women	60	1.0	750	15
Nursing Mothers	68	1.1	1,200	15
Old-age pensioners	50-60	0.7-0.9	750	10

Source: Jones (1988)

Retaining Nutrient Content of Foods

Dudek (2006) stated that even when it is carefully planned; an eating plan affords no guarantees that provides optimal amounts of nutrients especially if the food eaten has been improperly stored or overly processed. Generally, food begins to loose its nutrients the moment harvesting or processing begins; the more that is done to a food before it is eaten, the greater the nutrient loss. Heat, light, air, soaking in water, mechanical injury, dry storage and acidic or alkaline food processing ingredients can all hasten nutrient losses. Vitamins, minerals and fiber are particularly vulnerable to the effects of food processing.

Assessing Nutrition of Adults

Beaton *et al.* (1990) stated that nutritional assessment is a process that determines a client's nutritional status and the causes of any nutritional problems. The major purpose of a nutritional assessment is to determine the severity of nutritional impairment and probable causes. Nutritional assessment focus on information about dietary and anthropometric factors and the living environment of the client. Anthropometric screening is carried out through serial measurements of weight, height, mid upper arm circumference (MUAC). The values obtained are used to show changes in body mass and dimensions. According to Beaton *et al.* (1990), one way to assess the nutrition of adults is to calculate their body mass index (BMI). Adults with a BMI less than 18.5kg/m   indicates under-nutrition and high risk of illness; a BMI greater than 25kg/m ^{2} indicates risk of overweight; and a BMI greater than 30kg/m indicates obesity with a high risk of diabetes and heart disease. BMI is not applicable for pregnant women. Middle Upper Arm Circumference (MUAC) is the preferred measure.

Calculating body mass index (BMI)

BMI   = $\underline{\text{Weight in KG}}$
              (Height in Metres)

Example:

BMI   = $\underline{\hspace{1cm} 50 \hspace{1cm}}$
                    (1.60)   =   21Kg/m²

Measuring Body Composition Using (MUAC)

Young and Jaspers (2006) defined mid upper arm circumference (MUAC): Moderate malnutrition in adults is defined by a MUAC of less than 18.5cm with severe malnutrition being less than 16.0cm. A MUAC cut off point of <22cm is recommended for pregnant women. Low values are associated with under-nutrition (starvation or muscle wasting) and put a person at risk of illness. For children 1 to 5 years old, MUAC cut-off points are: 12.5-13.5cm indicating moderate under-nutrition; and <12.5 indicating moderate to severe malnutrition.

Special Meals in Prison

Bosworth (2004) noted that in most American systems, prisoners with medical conditions, such as diabetes, HIV & AIDs, pregnancy or heart problems, request special meals. Similarly, Vegans, who eat no animal byproducts, are increasingly becoming recognized as a legitimate group with special dietary needs.

Marquart and Roebuck (1987) noted that religious prisoners form another group who require and are usually entitled to special meals (Marquart and Roebuck, 1987) while some prisons provide different meals for each faith group, others, like the US Federal Bureau of Prisons, offer one uniform option known as "Common Fare" that tries to satisfy the dietary requirements of all religions. In this system, the meat is kosher, pork and its derivatives are never used, and vegetarian options are meant always to be available.

In order to avoid contamination with non-kosher or Halal food, Common Fare meals are usually served with disposable plates and cutlery (Marquart and Roebuck 1987). Certain other religious-based food requirements are usually honored throughout the year. Muslims may eat breakfast before dawn and eat dinner after sunset during Ramadan. All Jewish prisoners, who submit a request in writing to the Chaplain, are entitled to kosher food for Passover. Christians are offered a meatless meal on the mainline menu during Ash Wednesday and on all Fridays of Lent.

Johnson, (2008) stated that at the medical facility of Luzira Prison, Uganda's biggest penitentiary situated in a Kampala suburb, the sick inmates eat lunch comprising a bowl of *posho*, a flour and water based staple, and a bowl of the broth of bean soup without beans. They receive extra rations – soya, greens grown in the yard behind the facility, and tomatoes and onions from the central prison system.

Food as Punishment in Prisons

The Laws of Kenya, Prisons Act, Cap 90, section 51 (1a) gives the officers in charge powers to punish prisoners by confining them in a separate cell on a prescribed punishment diet. Burton, *et al.* (1998)

state that other than restricting access to the commissary, food may not, by law, officially be used as punishment. There is no longer any such thing as a diet of bread and water. Inmates, even when in disciplinary segregation, are entitled to nutritionally adequate meal. Ordinarily these are from the menu of the day for the institution. However, the same authors continue to allude that some super-maximum security facilities serve what is known as a 'food-loaf' or 'meal-loaf' to recalcitrant inmates, especially those who continually throw faeces or urine on staff. This product is made up of the ingredients of a regular meal, for example hotdogs, potatoes and beans that have been mashed together, baked like a meat loaf, and served. Although nutritionally adequate, and thus not equivalent to a diet of bread and water, in serving, taste and aesthetics, it functions as form of punishment, even if defined as a "dietary adjustment" (Burton, *et al.* 1998)

According to Wyke, (2007) at a prison that detains murderers and Mafiosi in Velletri, a small town south of Rome, in Italy, prisoners play an active role in cultivating organic fruit and vegetables and making fresh juices, jams, tomatoes, olive oil and wine. The prison has state-of-the-art food production zones including the latest computerised fertilising systems in its orchards, and micro-filtered wine-making equipment in its cantina. "The aim is to give detainees a useful skill to take with them when they leave prison," says Rodolfo Craia, an agronomist who oversees the teaching of small groups of prisoners who volunteer their work.

Ekwuruke, (2005) stated that in Nigeria, the statement of the Prison's Act No.9 of 1972 made it clear that prisons are not designed for the punishment of inmates but rather a move to identify the cause of their anti-social behaviors and to set in motion machineries for correcting their faults so that they may return to the society as useful and law abiding citizens.

According to Ogbozor, (2006) in Nigerian Prisons, punishment generally comes in the form of an order to do chores, such as washing the clothes of 'chiefs,' but often prisoners pay for misdeeds by being beaten or even sexually assaulted. Despite efforts by inmates to impose some sort of organisation, prison riots are common. Ogbozor, (2006) noted that in Nigeria riots in prisons across the country were all linked mostly to the lack of food for detainees.

Brown and Henkel, (2006) state that Sheriffs were responsible for providing meals with limited funds to prisoners, so no one worried about the kind of food being served, how it was prepared, or when it was served. Hiring the prisoners out to work was a way to raise money and cut feeding expenses. Brown and Henkel (2006), added that supervisors were forced to show a profit, so cuts were made. In many cases it has been the selection or quality of the prisoners' food. Minimal costs led to providing only bread, water, stew and porridge for many prisoners. Some sheriffs and deputies felt that limiting prison food was a good way to punish inmates. Food quality and servings are a common reason for prisoner unrest.

The Cultural Significance of Food

Beckford and Gilliat, (1998) noted that in prison, food creates or ameliorates conflict, establishes social boundaries of power and status, and provides a significant element in prisoner culture. Prison meals establish a routine for prisoners and staff. For most, however, meals provide a valued opportunity to interact with others. Beckford and Gilliat, (1998) went ahead and noted that the scarcity of desirable food in prison creates an illicit market for alternatives. As with other scarce resources, competition generates an underground acquisition and distribution system. Some food can be obtained from the prison kitchen by theft.

Beckford and Gilliat, (1998) continued to state that those who can acquire quantities of high-quality food use it as status-enhancing currency by sharing it with friends or impressing outsiders. Those particularly adept at obtaining quality merchandise develop a reputation as a valued peer. Pilfered food can be returned to the cellblock and distributed or sold, sometimes in collusion with staff. For well-connected inmates, quality food can be received from outside the prison.

Food Preparation in Prisons

According to Carlson and Garrett (1999), food is usually prepared according to a recipe system that the prison adopts. This recipe system ensures that the quantity and quality of meals are uniform and that staff issues do not enter into the preparation. Sanitation measures in the kitchen are absolutely critical. Each institution must have a daily cleaning and inspection system that ensures that the food preparation, storage, serving and dining areas are clean. The health of every inmate and staff member in the institution affects the cleanliness of the food service area. Each institution should consider having a hazard analysis critical control point system in place to ensure that proper food-handling procedures are being followed for receipt, storage, preparation, holding and serving of foods. This may help ensure that good personal hygiene and cleanliness are a focus for all food service staff and inmate workers. Adequate hand-washing facilities should be provided in the kitchen area. Clean uniforms and aprons should always be available and food handlers should be required to wear head coverings, hairnets and beard guards while cooking or serving food.

Donovan, (1982) noted that in four prisons and jails - the Mercer County Jail and the State Prison in Trenton, the Youth Correctional Institution in Annandale and the Correctional Institution for Women in Clinton - meals are prepared ''regethermically,'' a cook-chill system. Under that system, food for a seven-day week is cooked within a 40-hour, five-day week. What is not used immediately is blast-chilled to approximately 45⁰c in an insulated 250-cubic-foot steel cabinet.

Consequently, according to Donovan, (1982) after blast-chilling, the food is deposited in a food bank, where it is kept at 36⁰c, usually no longer than four days, although it can stay as long as seven days. It is withdrawn about 90 minutes before serving, and is reheated to the proper eating temperature in an infrared oven, a process that takes about 20 to 30 minutes.

Donovan, (1982) continues to explain that the central kitchen on the basement level of the Mercer County Jail is typical of where the regethermic system is used. It is the only central kitchen for the state's correctional facilities. Utensils, pots, pans and sinks are all oversized, trays are stacked in overhead racks and spoons and colanders hang from the ceiling. Donovan, (1982) adds that there are two regethermic ovens, each with a capacity for sixteen full-sized pans each pan holds enough food for 20 people. A chiller, which stands across from the ovens, can accommodate ten full pans. And the food bank, about 10 feet behind the chiller, can hold about fifty five racks, or two thousand pans.

Donovan (1982) notes further that correctional facilities that rely on the Mercer County Jail's central kitchen - for example, Annandale may run out of beef stew - get their supply via insulated regethermic carts that are transported in trucks. The carts can keep food at eating temperature for three hours, regardless of the outside temperature. According to Donovan, (1982) jails and prisons can order as much as four days' food, which they store and rethermalize in smaller regethermic appliances. These are about half the size of those in the central kitchen. Donovan (1982) stated that a regethermic kitchen is ideal when you have a mass feeding process.

Blast-chilling conserve the nutritional value of foods. Regethermic food preparation was begun in European hospitals about seventeen years ago. Time and money have been saved by adopting the concept of regethermic because stocks are purchased in mass quantity (Donovan 1982)

The regethermic kitchen permits a reduction of seventy two man-hours a week in the kitchen. Before, a seven-day week in the kitchen would consist of one hundred and twelve hours, with two shifts -one from 5 a.m. to 6 p.m. and the other from 10 p.m. to 6 a.m. Now, with a five-day week, we only need eight hours per day to prepare meals (Donovan 1982)

In Cuba, according to Oswaldo, (2008) both the condition of the kitchens in which prisoners' food is prepared and the food itself meet no acceptable standard. The schedule of food preparation is sporadic. Frequently there are long time lags between the food preparation and its consumption, the food is allowed to spoil, and in some cases the food is prepared with unsafe water. It is then served to prisoners who suffer from frequent digestive problems and severe stomach infections.

Ruzbeh and Bedi (2004) report that in Indian Prisons, food is cooked in prison, in make shift traditional style. For instance, three to four bricks are arranged to make a square, within which, either coal or if you are poor, then very often *roti* (hard traditional bread), is used as fuel to light a fire and to cook or heat food. Very often, dinner is served by 5.50 p.m. The food gets ice cold by night fall. By sunset, the inmates are all locked up in their cells. Thus, the food is normally heated in the cell itself. Often, prison food is not palatable, so it is modified, by adding spices and then transforming the dish into something that is reasonably edible. Often, those prisoners who have money don't touch prison food. They call for ration from outside and pay the poorer inmates to prepare a proper meal. The inmate is either paid in cash, kind or can partake of the food.

Chibvuri, (1997) noted that in Zimbabwe prisons, the kitchen conditions are shocking. They do not use hot water for washing and often there are no detergents to clean cooking utensils. Stainless steel containers used for meat are left greasy. Floors, toilets and dining tables are cleaned with filthy pieces of old blankets, and there are no brooms or hosepipes. Diarrhoea and other stomach disorders are rife, whilst broken toilets remain unserviceable for years.

Sanchez, (1994) stated that having prisoners to farm their own food saves money and also teaches prisoners that they can have productive lives. Prisoners prison maintenance such as laundry and food preparation. This keeps the prison costs down and keeps the inmates busy. Prisoners could construct their own housing and supply their own food. If they refuse to work, then they do not eat.

Carlson and Garrett (1999), recommend that food supplies and storage should be of the best quality possible within the institution's budget and of sufficient quantity to guarantee a wholesome diet. Some prison systems have food and farm operations that provide meat, vegetables, milk, grains and other items for their institutions. All food should meet or exceed government standards. The delivery and storage system should ensure that food supplies are fresh and delivered in suitable conditions. All incoming food not immediately used or processed in some way should be properly stored to prevent spoilage or waste. Proper storage should be available immediately for perishables such as meat, milk, eggs and fresh vegetables and fruits. Semi-perishable foods such as canned goods may be kept in temperature-controlled storage rooms. Shelf goods should be stored at 45°C (80°F), refrigerated foods at 35°F to 40°F, and frozen foods at 0°F or below. Each refrigerator or walk-in storage unit should have a thermometer on the door of the exterior wall so that staff can check these temperatures easily. Temperatures should be checked and recorded as required.

Food Service in Prisons

According to Flynn,.*et al.* (1998) the National Audit Office in Britain was less complimentary about the times of the day that food is served in prison, and about the fact that meals are often served more than two hours after being prepared. In order to accommodate staff working patterns, breakfast in most prisons is served at 8:00 a.m., lunch at 11:30 a.m. and the evening meal often as early as between 4 and 4:30 p.m. Flynn, *et al.* (1998), further stated that this contravenes the Prison Service standard of a maximum of 14 hours between evening meals and breakfast. As food is mostly served to prisoners in their cells and has to be wheeled on trolleys along corridors from the kitchens, by the time it reaches the cells it is sometimes either lukewarm or cold.

N.I.P.S., (2008) noted that in Northern Ireland, Prisoners complained about the timing of meals. The main meal is served at 3.30 p.m. and breakfast is served at 8.00 a.m. More than 16 hours between meals is excessive, they feel. Some also complained that meals consisted of too many high fat foods.

Carlson and Garrett, (1999) recommend that when a new prison is under construction, an important consideration is what type of serving system is used. The degree of staff supervision required and the institution design determine the system used for serving.

Food can be served cafeteria style or pre-plated and carted to the inmate. Both systems have their own challenges. Carlson and Garrett, (1999) believe that gathering a large number of inmates together in a cafeteria presents a security under any circumstances. The dining rooms create a potential site for serious disturbance and other incidents. As a result, in a cafeteria setting it is critical that correctional staff enforce an orderly system of food lines and seating as well as portion and utensil control.

Carlson and Garrett, (1999) stated that food should be served as soon as possible after preparation and at appropriate temperatures. Temperatures are ordinarily maintained by keeping the food in warmers of some type, either cabinet or pan style. Direct service is usually from a steam table or some other type of cafeteria-style warming equipment. Carlson and Garrett (1999) further stated that food distribution should be supervised at all times. Frequently, inmates serving food take advantage of an officer's temporary absence to take care of friends or not to give other inmates their entitled portions. Selection of eating utensils should be dictated by the type of population confined in an institution.

Oswaldo, (2008) stated that in Cuba, the utensils with which food is served are unhygienic, as are the personnel that prepare the food. They use the prisoners' own buckets to serve milk at breakfast; these same buckets are also used for bathing, washing, and emptying latrines. The kitchen does not have washbasins or sinks with water, and the trays on which they serve food are dirty and covered with grease. Oswaldo (2008) further stated that in addition, the containers for solid waste do not have lids, and this allows insects, bacteria, and all types of vectors of disease to proliferate. If the prisoners' food manages to avoid the dangers of preparation mentioned above, which is rare, the food is still prepared with no attention to taste.

Chibvuri, (1997) stated that in Chikurubi Maximum Security Prison in Zimbabwe, the food in prison is very meagre. Breakfast is at 8:30am, lunch 10:30am and supper 1:30pm. This leaves a 19-hour period every day without food.

Carlson and Garrett, (1999) stated that inmates should be given enough time to wash before eating. Inmates working outside or in other active occupations should be allowed to change clothing before entering the dining room. Random inmate searches for weapons and contraband should be performed. The dining rooms should provide normal group eating areas and permit conversation during dining hours. Whenever possible, there should be open dining hours to reduce the traditional waiting line. Serving and dining schedules should offer a reasonable amount of time for inmates to eat. Line cutting can become a problem in a crowded dining room. Close staff supervision can deter this activity and prevent major confrontations. The inmate dining room should not be used as a shortcut to other areas and inmates should not be allowed to linger in the dining area.

Number and Timing of Meals

According to Dudek (2006), all cultures eat at least once a day. Typically, Americans have three meals daily; Mexicans might have four to five meals daily. In some places in Africa, one meal per day is standard. When meals are eaten is also dictated by culture. Dinner takes place between 7pm and 9.00pm in Kenya and at approximately 6.00pm in Australia. A Lebanese custom is to arrive anytime when invited for dinner, even as early as 9.00am or 10.00am.

According to Edwards (2001) prisons in UK serve breakfast between 8.00-8.20 am, lunch between 12.00-12.20am and supper between 5.00-5.20pm.

Diet Scale

Sections 49 and 118 of the Prisons Act contain issues related to the administration of the diet scale or 'rations'. Details of these sections are discussed in this sub-section.

Contents of section 49:

49. (1) subject to the provisions of section 35 of the Act, every prisoner shall be entitled to a sufficient quantity of plain, wholesome Food in accordance with scale "A" in the First Schedule to these

Rules; Provided that regard shall be had to the mode and standard of life of a prisoner before he was admitted into prison and if the officer in charge after consultation with the medical officer is satisfied that a prisoner is not accustomed to the type of diet laid down in Scale "A" be given a diet in accordance with Scale B, Scale 'C" or Scale "D" in such Schedule.

(2) A copy of the diet scales shall be displayed in some conspicuous part of the prison.

(3) The diet of a prisoner who persistently wastes his food may be reduced by the officer in charge after obtaining the written advice of the medical officer.

(4) A prisoner ordered penal diet shall have substituted for his ordinary diet the penal diet set out in the First Schedule to these Rules unless the medical officer otherwise recommends.

Contents of section 118 states that "Persons performing work in a Government institution under an order made under section 68 of the Act shall receive a diet which shall be on the Scale A.2 in the First Schedule to these Rules."

Penal Diet

Penal diet is food given less than the normal daily ration. It is used as a punishment to prisoners for offences committed while in prison. Details of the penal diet are contained in the Prisons Act Cap 90 section 51 as detailed here under

51.(1) An officer in charge, if he is a senior prison officer or an administrative officer, may punish any prisoner found after due inquiry by him to be guilty of a minor offence by awarding him one or more of the following punishments -

(*a*) Confinement in a separate cell on the prescribed punishment diet for a term not exceeding such period as may be prescribed;

(2) An officer in charge, if a subordinate prison officer, may punish any prisoner found after due inquiry by him to be guilty of a minor

prison offence by awarding him one or more of the following punishments -

(*a*) Confinement in a separate cell on the prescribed punishment diet for a term not exceeding such period as may be prescribed;

(3) An officer in charge, if a senior prison officer or an administrative officer, may punish any prisoner found after due inquiry by him to be guilty of an aggravated prison offence by awarding him one or more of the following punishments

(*b*) Confinement in a separate cell on the prescribed punishment diet for a term not exceeding such period as may be prescribed;

The Prisons Act Cap 90 in the Laws of Kenya under sections 74, 49, 118 and 51 that govern the management of food to prisoners clearly outlines the menu items and the diet scale. It also prescribes the administration of the penal diet. However, there is need to review the laws that govern the management of prison food with a view to removing the aspect of using food as punishment and also the rations that seem to be inadequate for the various ages of prisoners and their physical needs. The menu also needs to be reviewed to reduce the monotony.

CHAPTER THREE

Research Methodology

Overview

This chapter discusses the research methodology used in carrying out this study.

Study Area

The study was undertaken at Eldoret Men, Ngeria Men, Eldoret Women, Kamiti Maximum and Langata Women's Prisons. Eldoret Men, Ngeria Farm Prison and Eldoret Womens Prisons are located in Uasin Gishu District. Uasin Gishu is one of the twenty administrative districts in Rift Valley Province. It borders Trans- Nzoia, Koibatek, Nandi, Lugari, Kakamega, Keiyo and Marakwet Districts. It is divided into six administrative divisions namely Kesses, Kapseret, Moiben, Ainabkoi, Soy and Turbo. Eldoret municipality has fairly well developed social economic infrastructure. Eldoret Men's Prison is situated along Iten road approximately 2 km from Eldoret town with a total number of 1,265 prisoners both ordinary, convicted and remand prisoners. Ngeria Farm Prison is located at Kesses off Nairobi road approximately 20 km from Eldoret town. It is a men's prison with a total number of 218 convicted prisoners all serving short sentences. Eldoret Women's Prison is adjacent to Eldoret Men's Prison with a total number of 187 prisoners both convicted and those under remand. Kamiti Maximum Prison is located in Kiambu district, Central province along Kiambu road approximately 30 km from Nairobi city centre with a population of 3,580 convicted prisoners. Langata Women's Prison is located on the southern part of Nairobi which is the capital city of Kenya, off Langata road approximately 15 km from the city centre. It is the only maximum women prison in Kenya with a total number of 580 convicted prisoners all serving long sentences. The total number of prisoners used in each of the selected prisons was derived from the respective lock up count registers during the time of study.

All prisons fall under the Kenya Prisons Service which is a Department in the Office of the Vice President and Ministry of Home Affairs. The notice boards at the gates of all the prisons stated the vision and mission statements of the department as "A correctional service of excellence in Africa and beyond" and their mission as "To contain offenders in humane safe conditions in order to facilitate responsive administration of Justice, Rehabilitation, Social Integration and Community Protection". It further stated the core functions of Kenya Prisons Service Department which included; 1): To contain and keep offenders in safe custody, 2): To rehabilitate and reform offenders in order to promote their opportunities for social reintegration, 3): To facilitate administration of justice and 4): To facilitate training of youthful offenders for their re-entry into the Societal life Stream.

Research Design

Research design is the arrangement of conditions for collection and analysis of data in a manner that aims to combine relevance to the research purpose with economy as procedure (Kothari, 2008). The study employed a descriptive survey research design. This approach sought to collect data without manipulating the research variables or the respondents in an attempt to find out the catering situation as it is in prison. The researcher chose descriptive survey research design since it enabled finding out the 'real' situation of the catering department as it is through investigation that does not allow manipulation of the study variables (Patton, 2000). Further, the researcher chose a survey design since the findings in the selected prisons would be used as a basis of reform in all prisons in the catering department in Kenya.

Participant observation methodology was also employed. The researcher visited the catering areas and participated in the food preparation and service process while observing the methods used for purposes of the study. The researcher took temperatures of food after cooking, before service, during service and at the end of the service. In addition, the researcher weighed the food being served to ascertain the weight of the portion of food served to prisoners.

Target Population

The main target units for analysis of the study were prisoners in the five selected prisons in Kenya. In addition, prison warders, storekeepers as well as the officers in charge of catering in the selected prisons were used to solicit for more information as regards catering in Kenyan prisons. The population of the study was prisoners under the Kenya Prisons Service. There are 91 Prisons in Kenya with a total number of approximately 44,977 prisoners. The target population comprised of prisoners from five selected prisons namely: Eldoret Men, Ngeria, Eldoret Women, Kamiti Maximum and Langata Womens prisons with a total number of 5,830 prisoners. Thirty four warders and five storekeepers and officers in charge of catering in the selected prisons were interviewed.

Sampling Frame

A sampling frame is a list, directory or index of cases from which a sample can be selected. It is important to note that the degree of generalization of a study depends on the accuracy of the sampling frame from which the sample was selected (Mugenda and Mugenda, 1999). The sampling frame for this study was prisoners drawn from five purposively selected prisons in Kenya with a total population of 5,830 prisoners.

Sample Size

Samples were drawn from the target population of five prisons: Eldoret Men, Ngeria Men, Eldoret Women, Kamiti Maximum and Langata Women's Prisons comprising 5,830 prisoners.

The sample size for this study was 387 prisoners, 34 Prison warders and the officers in charge of catering in the selected prisons. The sample size was statistically obtained by calculating the sample size from the five prisons purposively selected while adjusting to round off decimals to one person. (Mugenda's and Mugenda's, 1999) formula of calculating the sample size was applied.

$$Nf = \frac{n}{1 + n)/N}$$

Where:

Nf = the desired sample size (when the population is less than 10,000).

n=the desired sample size (when the population is more than 10,000).

N=the estimate of the population size.

Therefore, if the desired sample size is 384 when the population is more than 10,000, on a precision of 5% and a confidence level of 95% (Mugenda and Mugenda, 1999), the sample size for this study was attained a follows;

$$Nf = \text{less than } 10,000 = \frac{384}{1 + 384)/5830} = 362$$

Sampling Procedure

Sampling procedure is the process of deriving a sample from a given population according to certain rules. It is normally done with the keen understanding of the characteristics of a population including size, distribution and other features that distinguish the elements in the population to ensure all aspects of a population are captured in the selected sample.

This study involved the use of purposive sampling technique in which the researcher chose five prisons out of a total of 91 prisons for the study. The choice of the sampling technique was based on the convenience to the researcher in terms of availability of information. The sampling frame chosen had the required information with respect to the objectives of the study and the elements had the required characteristics. Additionally, because of security reasons and the dangerous nature of the respondents, Prison Warders randomly selected 387 prisoners from the five selected prisons for the study.

Data Collection and Instruments

Both primary and secondary methods of data collection were employed in this study. Questionnaires, structured interview schedules, observation schedules and conversations were used to collect primary data. Interviewing prisoners and prison warders generated the primary data. Primary data was collected through the administration of pre-tested researcher assisted questionnaires to the randomly selected prisoners in each prison, structured interviews to prison warders, participant observation schedules and conversations. These were the best tools for use since they reduced incidences of missing data and low rate of return. Data collection was carried out by the researcher and research assistants between 4th December 2008 and 15th January 2009. The questionnaires were administered by the researcher and seven research assistants to avoid missing data and misunderstanding of the questions by the respondents.

Administration of Research Instruments

On arrival at the selected prisons, the researcher accompanied by the research assistants, presented an authority letter from the Commissioner of Prisons which indicated that permission had been granted to undertake research at selected prisons. The research team, which comprised a maximum of seven members, underwent a thorough security screening process. Clearance was sought from senior authorities before gaining access to the prison premises. The data collection team was required to deposit identity cards, mobile phones and cameras at the gate before being allowed in the prison. The officer in charge assigned a prison warder to the team as a coordinator. Thereafter, a room was made available where the team set themselves up for data collection. The exercise kicked off at a slow pace on the first day mainly due to delays brought about by protocol and security issues.

Several batches of prisoners were randomly selected by prison warders and presented for interviews to the research team. Prisoners in the condemned section were not presented for interview because the prison authorities felt that they were dangerous criminals hence posed a great security risk to everyone. The questionnaires were written in English but sometimes necessitated translation into Kiswahili, depending on the education and language competence of the respondents. At all times during the exercise, at least three prison warders provided security to ensure and guarantee the safety of the research team. The questionnaires were researcher-administered and each took between 20-30 minutes to complete. The prisoners were very cooperative in answering the questions. During data collection, delays would be experienced mainly brought about by changes in shifts of the warders, interruptions emanating from having to give time to the prisoners to have their meals, roll call which was done on an hourly basis and to allow prisoners working outside the prison to return for some of them to be included in the sample.

In Eldoret Men and Kamiti Maximum Prisons, the data collection exercise took three days while in the other three sampled prisons it took only one day because the number of respondents' was small. Data collection took place between 9.30am – 5.00pm because access to the prison was restricted to that time. However, within the prison premises, there was free interaction and verbal exchange with the prisoners as long as it was within eyesight of the warders, and as long as none of the research team members ventured beyond the area allocated for data collection. In several instances, respondents tended to go out of topic by discussing their personal issues and it took the research team great tact and skill to divert them back to the subject matter of the study.

Interviews for prison warders were carried out at the same venue as that for the prisoners. However, collection of data from prison warders was very difficult as many of them feared that they would be victimized for information disclosed. However, it took the persuasion of the coordinating warder to convince them to accept to be interviewed. The storekeepers were interviewed outside the stores while the officers-in-charge were interviewed in their offices. Observation and taking of photographs was only allowed after permission was granted by the Kenya Prisons Service Department. The researchers were restricted to areas that were related to catering. Three researchers participated in the observation process. They were escorted by prison warders to observe the type of food, the preparation and service of food. During observation, the researchers participated in the food preparation process and paid attention to key areas such as the hygienic conditions of the kitchen area, the equipment and the persons cooking and serving food. In addition the ingredients that were used for cooking and the general conditions prevailing at the food and service areas were also observed. The researchers observed the service process and the place where food was eaten. In the process of observation, the researcher took notes and photographs of areas that were of importance to the study. All stores of the selected prisons were visited for observation on the storage conditions in terms of the temperature and facilities.

Conversations between the researchers and the prisoners that were relevant to the study were recorded as the prisoners voluntarily entered into open discussions.

Primary Data and Sources

First, primary data was obtained from 387 prisoners. The questionnaires were divided into five sections. In section A, the data collected included the respondents' socio-demographic characteristics such as age, level of education, marital status, religion, number of years in custody, gender, occupation before imprisonment and while in imprisonment. In section B, the data collected included the respondents' level of satisfaction with the type of food served such as the nutritive value of food, the sensory characteristics of food in terms of taste, odour, colour, texture and appearance of food and the purpose of food in prisons. In section C, the data collected included the perception of the respondents of how food is prepared such as the persons cooking the food, the methods of cooking, the equipment used in cooking, the time food is prepared, the quality of ingredients used in cooking and the hygienic conditions of the food preparation area. In section D, the data collected included the perception of the respondents' of food service in prisons such as the temperature of food served, quantity of food served, the time food is served, the equipment used in food service, the plates and mugs used, the hygienic conditions of the service area and the persons serving the food. In section E, the data collected included the respondent's perception of management supervision in catering issues such as the hygienic conditions, ensuring time of meals is kept and also ensuring that all prisoners get equal quantities of food.

Second, the researcher used structured interview schedules to collect data from thirty four warders from all the selected prisons to solicit more information on their views on prison food, the preparation and service of food and any other information that could contribute to the quality of catering services in prisons. Storekeepers and officers-in-charge of the selected prisons were also interviewed using interview schedules that contained both structured and unstructured questions. Information sought from storekeepers in the selected prisons was important in providing insight on such issues as procurement procedures, daily ration allocation and storage of food. The officers in charge gave information from the administrative point of view on such issues as budgetary allocations to the prisons to meet catering for inmates.

Third, the researcher used participant observation schedules to solicit more information on the objectives of the study. The researcher and research assistants participated actively in the process of food preparation and service in all the selected prisons. In addition the researcher weighed the food that was being served to the prisoners and took temperatures of the food after preparation, before service, during service and at the end of the service using a food thermometer. Visits to the catering areas included the kitchen and stores for direct observation which formed an important ingredient to the study. Further, the researcher took photographs of all aspects pertaining to catering in prisons. The researcher was assisted by two research assistants in conducting the observation schedules in the five prisons in order to familiarize herself with the catering aspects of the prisons as well as observe hygiene and other aspects that related to the study. Detailed notes were made from the observations and then coded thematically after sorting and summarizing the observation process.

Last, the researcher used conversations between the researcher, research assistants and prisoners and prison warders to gather additional information relevant to the study that was not covered in the questionnaires.

Secondary Data and Sources

Secondary data such as the Laws of Kenya *Prisons Act Cap 90*, "first schedule" which was used to compare the menu items stipulated and actual food consumed by prisoners was collected from the Kenya Prisons Service Department. Other secondary data collected included information on food preparation and service in prisons the world over and the menu items served to prisoners in different countries. The sources included libraries, the internet, publications, newspaper articles, journals, government press and Prisons Department. The data was used to provide background and supplementary information on catering services in prisons.

Secondary data gathered also contained information on the perception of quality of catering services, type of prison food in some parts of the world, prison menus, nutritional requirements of different people, retaining nutrient content of foods, assessing nutrition of adults using Body Mass Index (BMI), special meals in prison, food as punishment in prisons, the cultural significance of food, food preparation in prisons, food service in prisons, number and timing of meals, recommended servings and the Kenyan recommended prison food menu as stipulated in the Prisons Act Cap 90.

Pilot Test

A pilot test was conducted to test the reliability and validity of the data collection instruments. Bell (1999) and Mugenda and Mugenda (1999) allude that pilot testing of questionnaires assists in identifying deviance, finding out how long the questionnaire takes to complete, clarity of the instruction, questions that are unclear and attractive, suitable data analysis methods for the study and other comments. Kapsabet Prison was used by the researcher for the pilot study since it was not included in the unit of analysis for the research. The pilot test involved 15 prisoners (10 male and 5 female) and 4 prison warders of Kapsabet men and women prisons. This assisted in refining and revising data collection instruments.

Research assistants were thoroughly trained in the procedure of administering the questionnaires in prison. They accompanied the researcher in piloting and modifying the research instruments in order to comprehend fully the purposes and method of data collection. The researcher and the research assistants personally administered the questionnaires to the respondents and guided them by the questions in the interview schedule.

Data Analysis Procedure

Data obtained was mainly analysed quantitatively and qualitatively. Microsoft Excel package and Statistical Package for Social Sciences (SPSS) were used in data analysis. Both descriptive and inferential tests were performed. Descriptive methods included frequency distribution tables and percentages, pie charts and bar charts while inferential comprised multiple regression, independent samples t-test and one-way ANOVA.

Excel package was used to develop an index using the Likert scale for each of the three variables, type of food ($\overline{X_1}$), food preparation ($\overline{X_2}$) and food service ($\overline{X_3}$). The indices for the three variables were derived from the means of the responses of each respondent of the sub-variables. The sub-variables averaged to obtain type of food included the nutritive value of food, the sensory characteristics of food in terms of the taste, odour, colour, texture and appearance of food and the purpose of food which encompassed food reduced as punishment, food increased for sexual favours, food used as inducement, food for sustenance and food used as punishment.

The sub-variables averaged to derive food preparation included the time food is prepared, the equipment used to prepare food, the persons cooking food, the ingredients used and the conditions under which food was cooked, hygiene of the kitchen and the selection of persons to prepare food in terms of bad, unfair, favouritism, corrupt, commercial, as reward and tribalism.

The sub-variables averaged to obtain food service included the temperature of food, the persons service food, selection of the persons serving food, the equipment for serving, the methods of service, the time of service, place of eating, hygiene conditions of food service, plates and mugs used and the quantity of food served.

Multiple Regressions

Regression analysis is a type of analysis used when a researcher is interested in finding out whether an independent variable predicts a given dependent variable (Mugenda, Mugenda, 1999). In this study multiple regression was used to determine whether the independent variables (type of food, food preparation and food service) predict the dependent variable (quality of catering).

Multiple regression was also chosen by the researcher because the parameter estimates of multiple regression employ the method of Least Squares which are unbiased, exhibit least variance that are efficient, have Best Linear Unbiased (BLU), least mean square error and are sufficient.

The index for quality was derived from means of the respondents' general level of satisfaction on the quality of the type of food, the way food is prepared and served. The mean was regressed and tested against the value of the means of the independent variables.

T-tests were used to test the level of significance for the first three hypotheses. All the three explanatory variables were significant in the determination of the explained variable at 1% level of significance.

One-Way ANOVA

One-way ANOVA is an inferential statistic technique that tells whether the differences between observed means are likely to exist in the population from which the sample was drawn. It is also used in testing variance of two populations to determine if they are equal, and to simultaneously compare two or more population means. In this study, one-way ANOVA was used to compare the variance between food preparation in the selected male and female prisons in Kenya.

Independent Samples T-Test

Independent samples t-test is a test statistic used to establish if a sample mean from one group of cases differs significantly from another group of cases. Independent samples t-test differs from the normal t-student statistic that seeks to establish if a sample differs significantly from some arbitrary value as it assesses differences in means from two groups of cases.

According to Koutsoyiannis (1993), the t-test is appropriate if the variance of the parent population is unknown and the sample size is small such that n<30. Secondly, t-test could be applied provided that the parent population is normal. For the application of t-statistic normality is crucial.

Independent samples t-test was used in this study to test the variation between the menu items stipulated in the Prisons Act Cap 90 and the actual menu items served to prisoners which was the last objective of the study.

The Quality of Catering in Kenyan Prisons

CHAPTER FOUR

Data Analysis and Presentation

Overview

This chapter presents the results of analysis of factors affecting quality of catering in Kenyan prisons. It is subdivided into two sections; the first section presents results of descriptive analysis and the second section presents results of inferential statistics. The results and discussions are based on the questionnaire responses of 387 prisoners', interviews of 34 prison warders, 5 storekeepers and 5 officers-in-charge of the prisons selected for the study. The presentation includes the type of food served to prisoners, the methods of preparation and the service of food in the selected prisons.

The researcher also used observation schedules to find out exactly the type of food served to prisoners, the preparation of food and service of food as it was in prisons. Observations in each of the variables were noted and reported graphically as part of the descriptive data.

In addition, during the course of the data collection, some prisoners held discussions with the researchers and voluntarily expressed their own views on the quality of catering. These comments were listened to so that the trust and understanding of prisoners involved could be gained. The comments made were either quite general or related to specific personal preferences. However the conversations between the researcher and respondents that were relevant to the study were noted at the back of questionnaires and some were reported in this section.

The Response Rate

The study targeted 362 respondents but 387 managed to fill the questionnaires. None of the questionnaires were spoilt therefore all the questionnaires were used in the analysis hence the response rate yielded 106.9% as the researcher had extra twenty five copies of questionnaires incase some got spoilt of which none did. Under normal research circumstances, the response rate is about 70%. This unusually high response was attributed to the use of researcher assisted questionnaires which enabled the researcher to clarify questions to the respondents hence their ability to respond to all questions. In addition, the prisoners had a positive attitude towards the questionnaires as they felt it provided an avenue for them to express their opinion on the state of catering in prisons and they also felt that it gave them a break to interact with people from the society. The prisoners also viewed the exercise with a hope coming change. The fact that the respondents are in a restricted area, they had all the time to participate in the data collection exercise. However, the accuracy level was good and eventually resulted in more questionnaires answered.

Descriptive Statistics

Descriptive statistics are used to describe the basic features of data in a study. They provide simple summaries about the sample and the measures together with simple graphics analysis. They form the basis of virtually every quantitative analysis of data. The primary use of descriptive statistics is to describe information or data through the use of numbers and to give a clear view of raw data by presenting quantitative descriptions in a manageable form.

Personal Information of Prisoners

The respondents profile was established by asking them for the information carried in the questionnaires. This information was solicited in order to break the ice between the researcher and respondents before asking questions related to the study. Further it was to provide the researcher with knowledge on the personal characteristics in order to get a clear picture of the type of respondents. This specifically focused on age, gender, marital status, highest level of education and religion as shown in table 4.1. The sample characteristics captured the respondent's number of years in custody and place where they lived prior to imprisonment. The respondent's employment status before imprisonment and their current duties in prison were also recorded. In addition, the respondent's weight in kilograms and height in meters were taken in order to obtain the respondents BMI. An ordinary bathroom weighing scale was used to measure the weight while a measuring tape was used to measure the height. The descriptive results in table 4.1 indicate that 77.8% of the respondents were male (n=301) while 22.2% were female (n=86). The majority of the respondents belonged to the age group between 31-40 years (n=113, 29.2%) while the least respondents belonged to the age bracket of above 40 years (n=79, 20.4%). The majority of respondents marital status and level of education as primary registered close frequencies of (n=211, 54.5% and n=205, 53%) respectively, showing a coherence of these two factors among the prisoners. A majority of the respondents were self-employed before imprisonment (n=196, 50.6%) and most of the respondents lived in their own house and rented houses before imprisonment (46.3% and 34.6%) which totals to 80.9%. The religion of most respondents indicated that they were Catholic's and protestant's (35.9% and 48.6%) which totals to 84.5% of the prisoners interviewed. A majority of those interviewed had served in prison for less than five years (74.2%). The frequencies and percentages of all results on personal information are all shown on table 4.1.

From the personal information of the prisoners obtained in table 4.1, the researcher was confident that the respondents were capable of adequately completing the questionnaires. Of the 387 prisoners interviewed, 74.2% were of 26 years and above and 54.5% of them were married. The level of education of majority of the respondents indicated that 89.4% of them had some basic education, 82.9% of them had some form of employment before imprisonment and 88.4%

of them were independent in terms of residence before imprisonment. From this information, it is clear that most of the prisoners interviewed had some kind of experience in catering and were therefore aware of quality of services. Therefore, the prisoners could easily discern changes in the quality of services and hence the researcher was confident of the respondent's capabilities in adequately providing the correct responses in the questionnaires.

With the personal information of the prisoners on table 4.1, the researcher was confident that the respondents provided information relevant for the study.

Table 4.1: Personal information of prisoners in prisons, 2009.

Name of Variable		Frequency	Percent
Prisons' Name	Eldoret men	89	23.0
	Ngeria Farm	33	8.5
	Eldoret women	28	7.2
	Kamiti	179	46.3
	Langata women	58	15.0
Age	Below 25 years	100	25.8
	26-30 years	95	24.5
	31-40 years	113	29.2
	Above 40 years	79	20.4
Gender	Male	301	77.8
	Female	86	22.2
Marital Status	Married	211	54.5
	Single	147	38.0
	Widowed	9	2.3
	Divorced	8	2.1
	Separated	12	3.1
Level of Education	None	41	10.6
	Primary	205	53.0
	Secondary Dropout	57	14.7
	O' Level	62	16.0
	A' Level	4	1.0
	College	12	3.1
	University	6	1.6
Employment before	Employed	125	32.3
Imprisonment	Self employed	196	50.6
	Unemployed	66	17.1
Duties in Prison	Industry	94	24.3
	Cooking	24	6.2
	Manual jobs	56	14.5
	Handwork & Dress making	86	22.2
	House hold & Cleaning	45	11.6
	Community	5	1.3
	Electrical & Mechanical	13	3.4
	Teaching, Artist & Library	7	1.8
	None	57	14.7
Number of years in	Below 2 years	143	37.0
CustodyBelow 2	2 - 5 years	144	37.2
Years	5 - 10 years	75	19.4
	Above 10 years	25	6.5
Residence before	Own own	179	46.3
Imprisonment	Rented House	134	34.6
	Housed by Employer	12	3.1
	Streets	17	4.4
	Parents / Friends	45	11.6
Body Mass Index	0 - 18	13	3.4
(KG/Msq)	18 - 25	277	71.6
	25 - 30	70	18.1
	Above 30	27	7.0
Religion	Catholic	139	35.9
	Muslim	52	13.4
	Protestant	188	48.6
	Other	8	2.1

Source: Researcher's own compilation, 2009.

Type of Food

The study sought to establish the type of food served to prisoners. With respect to the type of food in table 4.2, respondents indicated their views on the sensory characteristics of food, nutritive value of food and the purpose to which they attach prison food. The researcher has presented detailed descriptive results on three indicators; the nutritive value of food, the purpose of food and the sensory characteristics of food.

Table 4.2: Type of food in prisons, 2009

	Views on Aesthetic and Nutritive Value of food									
Name of Variable	V. Bad		Bad		Avg		Good		V. Good	
	Fq	%	Fq	%	Fq	%	Fq	%	Fq	%
a	General view on type of food in prisons	154	39.8	136	35.1	78	20.2	14	3.6	5	1.3
b	Taste of food	141	36.4	182	47.0	40	10.3	18	4.7	6	1.6
c	Oduor of food	115	29.7	172	44.4	68	17.6	24	6.2	8	2.1
d	Texture of food	124	32.0	172	44.4	58	15.0	25	6.5	8	2.1
e	Colour of food	97	25.1	180	46.5	68	17.6	34	8.8	8	2.1
f	Appearance of food	165	42.6	175	45.2	28	7.2	13	3.4	6	1.6
g	Nutritive value of food	144	37.2	175	45.2	42	10.9	20	5.2	6	1.6
h	Average	134	34.7	170	44	55	14.1	21	5.5	7	1.7
	Purpose of food in prison									
Name of Variable	Always		V. Often		Often		Rarely		Never	
	Fq	%	Fq	%	Fq	%	Fq	%	Fq	%
i	Food reduced as punishment	110	28.4	35	9.0	61	15.8	68	17.6	113	29.2
j	Food increased for sexual	165	42.6	57	14.7	18	4.7	22	5.7	125	32.3
k	Food used as inducement	69	17.8	40	10.3	43	11.1	65	16.8	170	43.9
l	Food for sustenance	323	83.5	14	3.6	16	4.1	7	1.8	27	7.0
m	Food denied as punishment	20	5.2	17	4.4	30	7.8	66	17.1	254	65.6
n	Average	137	35.5	33	8.4	34	8.7	46	11.8	138	35.6

Source: *Researcher's own compilation, 2009.*

From table 4.2 (h) above, 78.7% which accounts for the majority of the prisoners interviewed, they felt that the type of food in prisons, the sensory characteristics and nutritive value of food were *bad* to *very bad*. 14.1% felt that it was *average* while a minority of 7.2% felt that it was either *good* or *very good*. Interviews on the purpose of food in prison revealed that 83.5% of prisoners felt that food was just for sustenance as table 4.2(1).

Observations made by the researcher on the type of food served in prisons revealed that in all the prisons sampled, *ugali* was served on a daily basis as in plate 4.1(c). In one of the prisons, *ugali* was served with salty water as vegetables in plate 4.1(d) while in most of the prisons *ugali* was served with no vegetables or very little vegetables with a lot of watery soup that looked like dirty water as shown in plate 4.1(a). Beans were served with *ugali* in all the prisons with water (plate 4.1, b).

Plate 4.1: Watery vegetable and beans in prisons, 2009

Source: Author's own compilation, 2009

In Langata prison, '*githeri*' was served twice a week. In Ngeria, Eldoret women and Langata prisons, rice was served at least once a week. In the researcher's opinion, Eldoret men and Kamiti Maximum prisons served a very monotonous menu of *ugali* for lunch and supper on a daily basis. In all the prisons sampled, porridge was served for breakfast daily while meat was served at least three times a week. Prisoners who were lucky got at least two pieces of meat otherwise majority were served with meatless bones. Only Langata women prison served a semi-varied menu.

Nutritive Value of Food

It was found out that, of the 387 respondents, 37.2% of the prisoners sampled felt that the nutritive value of the food served to them was *very bad*, 45.2% felt the food served to them was *bad*, 10.9% thought the food was *average*, 5.2% felt it was *good* and only 1.6% said the nutritive value of food served to them was *very good* as shown on table 4.2(g). This makes it clear that most prisoners perceived the nutritive value of food served to them to be *bad* to *very bad* with a percentage totaling to 82.4% which means the nutritive value of food was poor (figure 4.1).

Additionally, within the respective selected prisons, the percentages for *very bad* nutritive value were 43.8%, 33.3%, 35.7%, 44.1% and 8.6% respectively. Kamiti Maximum prison had the highest percentage of those who perceived nutritive value to be *very bad* as shown in figure 4.1.

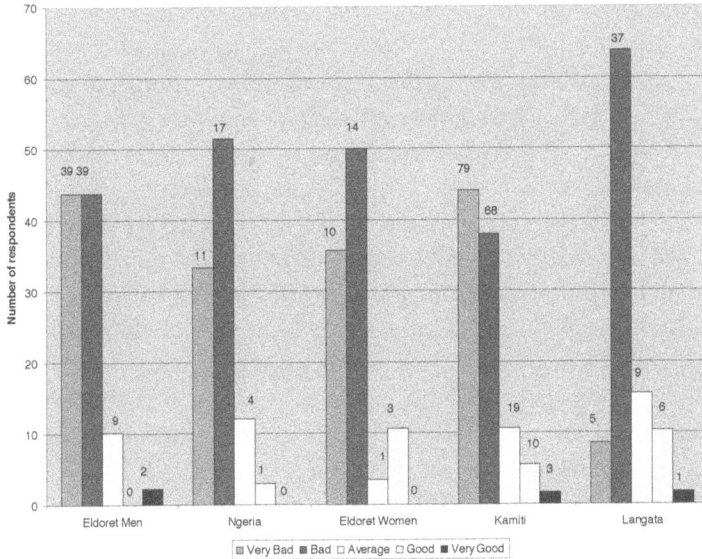

Figure 4.1: Prisoner's views on nutritive value of food in prisons, 2009.

Source: Researchers' own compilation, 2009

The percentages for *'bad'* were 43.8%, 51.5%, 50%, 38% and 63.8% respectively for the prisons as mentioned above. Langata women prison had the highest percentage of those who perceived the nutritive value of food served to be bad. The respective percentages of *average, good and very good* within the respective prisons can be obtained directly from figure 4.1.

Worth to note was the fact that a very small percentage of those interviewed felt the nutritive value of the food served was *good* or *very good* with some prisons like Eldoret men, Ngeria and Eldoret women reporting zero percentages in the categories, *good and very good.* With these results, the general feeling of most prisoners was that the nutritive value of food was *bad* to *very bad* hence, it can thus be generalized that indeed the nutritive value of food was poor.

Observations made by the researcher on the nutritive value of food indicated that it was poor and in effect seemed to be inadequate. The vegetables served were not adequate to provide all the necessary vitamins and there was no other source of vitamins in the food provided. Furthermore, the vegetables were boiled for long which resulted in loss of the necessary nutrients. The only source of vegetable protein was from beans while the few pieces of meat given to some prisoners were not adequate to provide animal protein. The weight of the meat served was 50g per piece which meant that each prisoner 'got' 100gms per week which was inadequate. Vegetable oil was provided in all meals whereby, in Ngeria, Eldoret women and Langata prisons, the oil was cooked in the food but in Kamiti Maximum and Eldoret men's prisons, oil was served separately from food such that, a prisoner was served *ugali* then the 'vegetable' followed by a spoonful of oil as shown on plate 4.2 (a & b). Carbohydrates served seem to be the only nutrient adequately provided to prisoners.

(a) (b)

Plate 4.2: Oil served in Kamiti Maximum Prison, 2009

Source: Author's own compilation, 2009

The Purpose of Food in Prison

Food in prison was served for different purposes some which were genuine while others could raise eyebrows in the public eye. Some of the purposes of food in prison included food for sustenance, food reduced for punishment, no food as punishment, food increased for inducement such as soliciting information and food increased for sexual favours.

Food increased for sexual favours was particularly interesting and drew the eye of the researcher to report on it as shown on table 4.3. From the table, 42.6% of the total number of prisoners interviewed were of the view that food was *always* increased for sexual favours. A further 14.7% of the prisoners felt that food was *very often* increased for sexual favours. These two categories combined gave a cumulative percentage of 57.3% of the prisoners who strongly felt that food was increased for sexual favours.

Further, 4.7% of the prisoners felt that food was *often* increased for sexual favours while 5.7% felt that food was *rarely* increased for sexual favours. Within the respective prisons, the percentages of those who felt food was *always* increased for sexual favours were 68.5%, 0%, 3.6%, 56.4% and 3.4% respectively. Eldoret men recorded the highest percentage of 68.5% followed closely by Kamiti Maximum with a percentage of 56.4%. Ngeria Farm prison recorded the smallest number of those who felt that food was *always* increased for sexual favours with a percentage of zero (0%). The percentages for *very often*, *often* and *rarely* for every respective prison can be obtained directly from table 4.3.

The percentage of those who felt that food was *never* increased for sexual favours were 4.5%, 75.8% and 85.7%, 16.2% and 74.1% respectively as enlisted on table 4.3. The conclusion drawn was that the behaviour of increasing food for sexual favours was rampant in Eldoret men and Kamiti Maximum prisons. The behaviour was less rampant in Eldoret women, Ngeria and Langata prisons.

Table 4.3: Food increased for sexual favours in prisons, 2009

Prisons Name	Food Increased for Sexual Favours										TOTAL
	Always		Very Often		Often		Rarely		Never		
	Fq	%	Fq	%	Fq	%	Fq	%	Fq	%	
Eldoret Men	61	68.5	19	21.3	2	2.2	3	3.371	4	4.5	89
Ngeria	0	0.0	1	3.03	2	6.1	5	15.2	25	76	33
Eldoret Women	1	3.6	0	0	0	0.0	3	10.7	24	86	28
Kamiti	101	56.4	31	17.3	9	5.0	9	5.0	29	16.2	179
Langata	2	3.4	6	10.3	5	8.6	2	3.4	43	74.1	58
Total	165		57		18		22		125		387
Percentage	42.6		14.7		4.7		5.7		32.3		

Source: Researcher's own compilation, 2009.

A further conclusion can be made that the behaviour of increasing food for sexual favours was more observed in male prisons than female prisons as shown in table 4.4 where 53.8% of male prisoners felt that food was *always* increased for sexual favours while an additional 16.9% of male prisoners felt that food was *very often* increased for sexual favours giving a cumulative percentage of 70% of those who had the strong feeling that food was increased for sexual favours. Only 3.5% of the female prisoners thought that food was *always* increased for sexual favours and a further 7.0% thought it was *very often* increased for sexual favours which gave a cumulative percentage of 10.5% of the women who strongly felt that food was increased to gain sexual favours from inmates. Table 4.4 presents a summary with regards to gender and increasing food for sexual favours among the prisons polled.

Table 4.4: Gender, prison and food for sex cross tabulation in prisons, 2009.

Gender	Prisons Name	Always	Very Often	Often	Rarely	Never	Total
Male	Eldoret Men	61	19	2	3	4	89
	Ngeria	0	1	2	5	25	33
	Kamiti	101	31	9	9	29	179
	Total	162	51	13	17	58	301
	%age	53.8	16.9	4.3	5.6	19.3	
Female	Eldoret Women	1	0	0	3	24	28
	Langata	2	6	5	2	43	58
	Total	3	6	5	5	67	86
	Percentage	3.5	7.0	5.8	5.8	77.9	

Source: Researcher's own compilation, 2009.

Observations made by the researcher reveal that the purpose of food increased for different reasons evidenced by the fact that when the researcher visited the kitchens in most prisons, small amounts of food were being cooked separately in '*mururus*' which in essence implied that there was some food kept aside for 'special' prisoners. That food was only comparable to food served in a hotel and greatly contrasted the food served to prisoners. Furthermore, conversations held with prisoners indicated that food was used by cooks for sexual favours either by increasing food as reward for sexual favours or decreasing food for a prisoner by a cook in order to force and entice the prisoner into being a sexual partner.

Sensory Characteristics of Food

Sensory characteristics of food encompassed aspects such as taste, odour, texture, colour and appearance of food. The rankings of these aspects were averaged to give a general picture of the sensory characteristics of food in prisons as perceived by the prisoners themselves with reference to all the five prisons as shown in figure 4.2.

From figure 4.2, it was established that 26.1% of all the respondents felt that the sensory characteristics of food was *very bad* while 56.6% interviewed felt that the sensory characteristics of food in prison was *bad*. These categories, *very bad and bad* had a total percentage of 82.7%. This was a clear indication that indeed the sensory characteristic was generally *bad* and thus the aspects of taste, odour, texture, colour and appearance of food were perceived to be *bad to very bad* by majority of the respondents. 12.4% of respondents felt that the sensory characteristics of food was *average*, 3.6% felt it was *good* and only 1.3% felt that the sensory characteristics of food was *very good*. The researcher took note of the fact that most of the respondents who felt that the sensory characteristics of food was *good* or *very good* worked as cooks in prison.

Within the individual respective prisons, the largest percentage of those who viewed the sensory characteristic as *very bad* were from Eldoret men prison with a percentage of 32.6% followed by Kamiti Maximum Prison with a percentage of 31.3%. At least 50% in all the five prisons sampled felt that the sensory characteristics of food were *bad*. Very few prisoners felt that the sensory characteristics of food was either *good* or *very good* with some prisons polling zero percentages in these two categories as can be seen from figure 4.2.

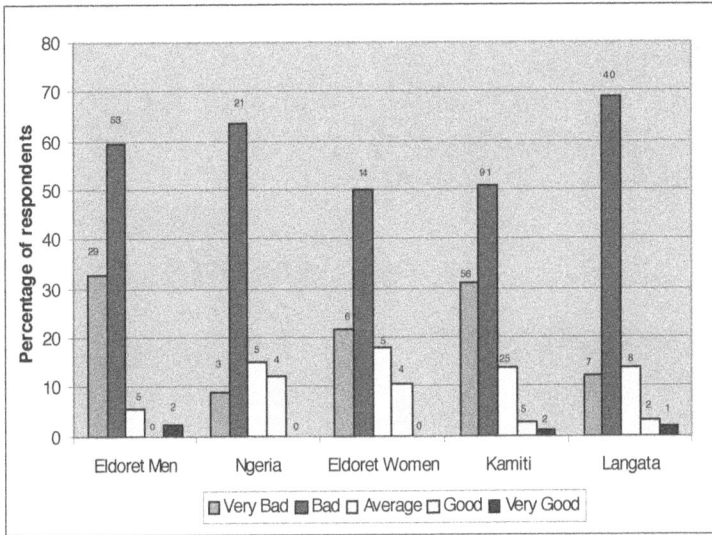

Figure 4.2: Sensory characteristics of food in prisons, 2009
Source: Researcher's own compilation, 2009.

Observations by the researcher revealed that the sensory characteristics of food in terms of appearance, colour, odour, taste and texture were poor. The colour of *ugali* looked pale as in plate 4.3 (a - f). The taste of *ugali* in most of the prisons was bitter, sour and fermented whereas the texture varied from prison to prison. The appearance of *ugali* in Eldoret Men's prison is as shown in plate 4.3 (a&b). The texture of *ugali* in Eldoret Men's Prison was too soft just like porridge left to harden and was lumpy and uncooked, such that it could be scooped from one container and poured to another as shown in plate 4.3 (c). On the other hand, Kamiti Maximum was on the extreme with hard texture and the appearance of *ugali* had yellow patches suggesting low quality of ingredients as shown on plate 4.3 (d). The texture of *ugali* in Langata prison was poor as shown in plate 4.3 (e & f). The aesthetic value of *ugali* in Ngeria and Eldoret women prisons was good.

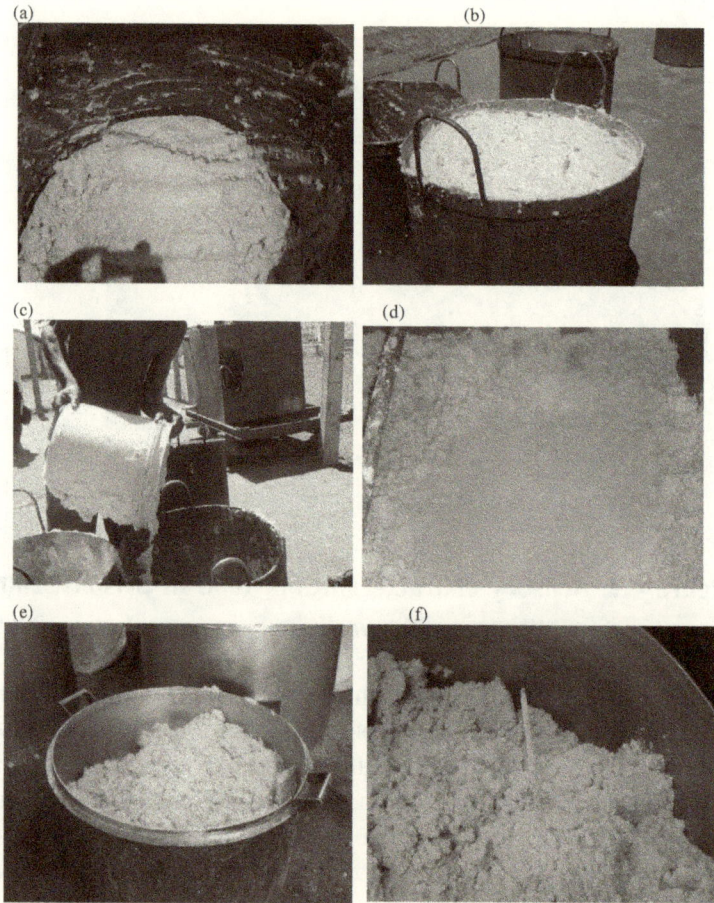

**Plate 4.3: Texture, colour and appearance of ugali in
prisons, 2009**

Source: Author's own compilation, 2009.

The appearance of vegetables was very unappetizing in all the prisons. In Eldoret Men's prison the appearance of bean soup was very unappetizing looking like dirty brown water as shown in plate 4.4(a). In Ngeria Farm Prison, the vegetables were cut into big pieces, overcooked to the point that the colour changed and presented with too much water as shown on plate 4.4 (b&c). In Eldoret women's prison, vegetables were also over cooked and again presented with too much water which made it extremely unappetizing as shown in plate 4.4 (d). In Kamiti Maximum and Langata Women Prisons, the vegetables were cooked and served whole such that the appearance was very unappetizing. The colour of vegetables in Kamiti was green and looked raw as shown in plate 4.4(e) while that of beans looked very unappetizing as in plate 4.4 (f). Vegetables in Langata Prison were overcooked and appeared very unappetizing as shown in plate 4.4 (g&h).

(a)

(b)

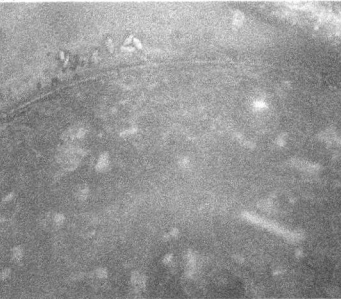
(c)

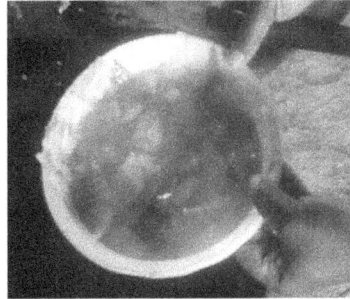
(d)

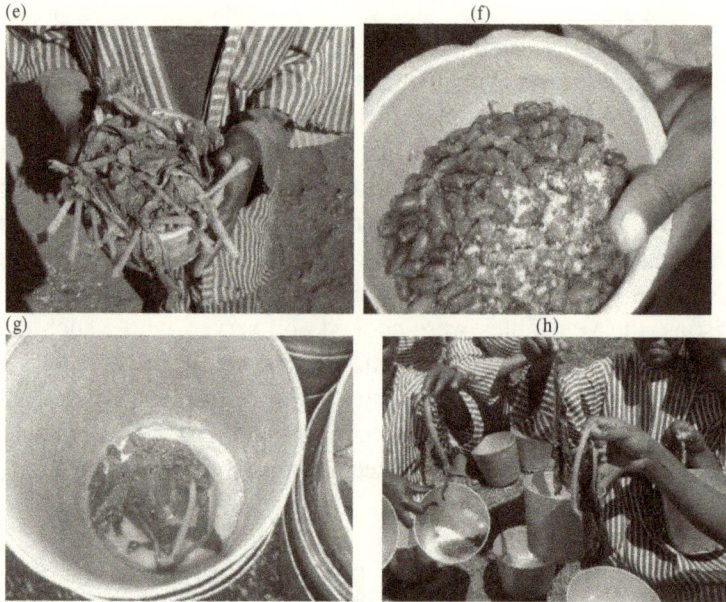

Plate 4.4: Texture, colour and appearance of vegetables in prisons, 2009

Source: Author's own compilation, 2009.

Preparation of Food

The researcher sought to establish food preparation practices and generally the way food was prepared in Kenyan prisons. The important aspects as far as food preparation in prisons was concerned included the persons cooking the food, the way food was cooked, the conditions under which food was prepared, the time food was prepared and the equipment used for preparing food. The response for variables under preparation of food are summarized in table 4.5.

Table 4.5: Food preparation, selected prisons, 2009.

Name of Variable	V. Bad		Bad		Average		Good		V.Good	
	Fq	%	Fq	%	Fq	%	Fq	%	Fq	%
General way food is cooked	124	32.0	147	38.0	73	18.9	59	15.2	16	4.1
Persons cooking food	126	32.6	113	29.2	73	18.9	59	15.2	16	4.1
Hygiene of food preparation	122	31.5	145	37.5	65	16.8	47	12.1	8	2.1
Time food is prepared	87	22.5	142	36.7	73	18.9	67	17.3	18	4.7
Equipment used in cooking	155	40.1	138	35.7	50	12.9	32	8.3	12	3.1
Average	123	31.7	137	35.4	67	17.3	53	13.6	14	3.6

Source: Researcher's own compilation, 2009.

From the average responses on food preparation shown in table 4.5 above, 67.1% of the respondents interviewed were of the opinion that food preparation was *bad* to *very bad*, another 17.3% felt that it was *average* while a minority of 17.2% felt that it was either *good* or *very good*. It can thus be concluded that food preparation in prisons was poor.

Persons Cooking Food

The general view of prisoners was collected on their opinion of how the persons cooking food were in terms of their relationship with other prisoners, the way they handled food preparation, the way they conducted themselves and generally the way they perceived them. Figure 4.3 gives a summary of how the persons cooking food were ranked in various prisons.

Table 4.5, shows 32.6% of all the respondents were of the opinion that the persons cooking food were *very bad*. 29.2% felt that the persons cooking food were *bad*. The *'very bad'* and *'bad'* gave a total percentage of 61.8% giving the indication that most prisoners were of the opinion that the persons cooking food were *bad*. 18.9% felt that the persons cooking food were *average*, 15.2% were of the view that they were *good* while 4.1% viewed the cooks as *very good*. The percentage of those who viewed cooks as *good* and *very good* added up to only 19.3%.

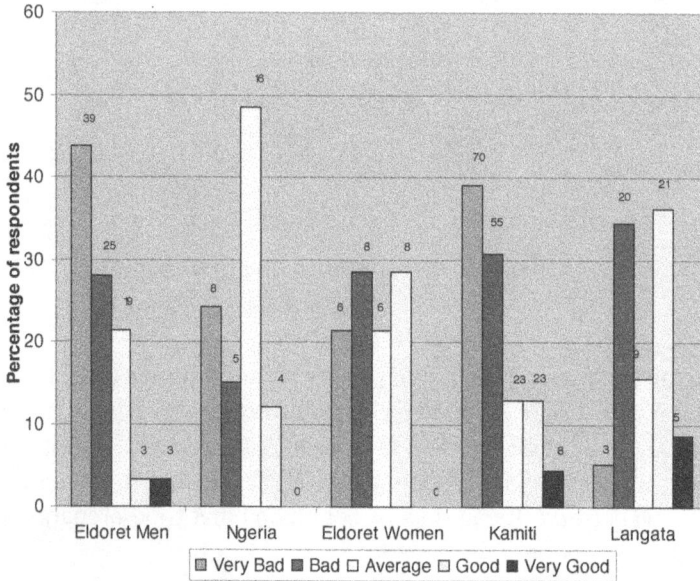

Figure 4.3. Persons cooking food in prisons, 2009
Source: Researcher's own compilation, 2009.

Within the individual prisons, 43.8% of prisoners in Eldoret men felt
that the cooks were *very bad*, 24.2% in Ngeria, 21.4% in Eldoret
women prison, 39.1% in Kamiti Maximum prison and 5.2% in
Langata women's prison. The percentages of those who viewed
cooks as *bad* were 28.1%, 15.2%, 28.6%, 30.7% and 34.5%
respectively. The percentages of those with the opinion that cooks
were *good* were 3.4%, 12.1%, 28.6%, 12.8% and 36.2%
respectively. In the *'very good'* category, the percentages were
3.4%, 0%, 0%, 4.5% and 8.6% respectively.

The feeling the researcher got from the above responses was that the persons cooking food in prison were bad with 61.8% of prisoners in support and only 19.3% of prisoners held a contrary opinion of the cooks.

Observations made on the persons cooking food revealed that they were healthy people who seemed to be happy with their jobs as they seemed to derive a lot of happiness from it. Further observations showed that they were not hygienic in the way they handled food plus their personal hygiene was of great concern. They wore torn clothes which were either prison uniforms or their personal clothes. Taking pictures of prisoners cooking was restricted.

The researcher established that most of the persons cooking food in Eldoret Men, Ngeria and Kamiti Maximum Prisons did not undergo medical examinations before they were allowed to cook food. This concern was raised by majority of the prisoners interviewed. In addition to the above, conversations with prisoners alleged that most of the cooks and food service prisoners were HIV positive. They further alleged that in some instances prisoners serving food got bruised and bled in the process of serving but continued to serve despite drops of blood dripping onto the food. Conversations held by the researcher and prisoners revealed that cooks were the biggest perpetrators ("*mende*") of homosexuality to the extent that some had upto 15 'girlfriends', who were referred to as '*watoto*'.

Further allegations were made that receptionists at the prison who received and allocated duties overstayed in one prison such that when prisoners were released, they were always able to make their way back to prison by breaking the law and on return, were allocated the same duties they served during their previous sentence hence they continued with 'business as usual'.

The Quality of Catering in Kenyan Prisons

Conditions under which Food was Prepared

The study found that 31.5% of all the prisoners interviewed were of the view that conditions under which food was cooked in prison was *very bad*. Overall percentage of 37.5% prisoners felt that the conditions were *bad*, 16.8% said the conditions were *average*, 12.1% felt the conditions were *good* while 2.1% were of the opinion that the conditions were *very good*. Upto 69% of the respondents were of the feeling that the conditions of food preparation were *bad* as compared to 14.2% of the respondents who viewed the condition of food preparation as being *good*. The conditions under which food was prepared in prison was generally thought to be poor by prisoners as shown in table 4.6 below.

Table 4.6: Conditions under which food was prepared in prisons, 2009

Prisons Name	Conditions under which food was cooked										TOTAL
	Very Bad		Bad		Average		Good		Very Good		
	No.	%	No.	%	No.	%	No.	%	No.	%	
Eldoret Men	36	40.4	34	38.2	12	13.5	4	4.5	3	3.4	89
Ngeria	4	12.1	13	39.4	7	21.2	9	27.3	0	0	33
Eldoret Women	3	10.7	10	35.7	10	35.7	5	17.9	0	0	28
Kamiti	71	39.7	70	39.1	26	14.5	9	5.0	3	1.7	179
Langata	8	13.8	18	31.0	10	17.2	20	34.5	2	3.4	58
Total	122		145		65		47		8		387
Percentage	31.5		37.5		16.8		12.1		2.1		

Source: Researcher's own compilation, 2009.

In the respective prisons, the percentages for *very bad* conditions were 40.4%, 12.1%, 10.7%, 39.7% and 13.8% respectively. For the *good* category the percentages were 38.2%, 39.4%, 35.7%, 39.1% and 31.0% respectively. Few prisoners thought that the conditions were *good* with the following percentages;- 4.5%, 27.3%, 17.9%, 5.1% and 34.5% respectively. In the *'very good'* category,

Ngeria and Eldoret women polled 0%, Eldoret men and Langata women each polled 3.4%, while Kamiti Maximum polled 1.8%.

Observations made on the conditions under which food was cooked in prison revealed that in all the prisons sampled, the kitchens' were poorly ventilated to the extent that a lot of smoke was retained in the kitchen. Furthermore, all the kitchen roofs had big holes and as such leaked during the rainy season as shown in plate 4.5 (a&b). The kitchen in Kamiti Maximum Prison had an open air space between the preparation section and service as shown on plate 4.5 (c). The kitchen roof in Langata Womens Prison at the time of data collection was very bad but it had been replaced at the time the researcher took photographs as shown on plate 4.5 (d). Apart from ventilation, most of the kitchens were dark, the walls have turned black and there was insufficient lighting as shown in plate 4.5 (e & f). In most of the prisons sampled, the kitchen space was inadequate for the population of prisoners' being cooked for and also the number of prisoners cooking. The '*jikos*' were fitted too close to each other which reduced space for proper and easy cooking as per plate 4.5 (g). Furthermore, the '*jikos*' used were not adequate compared to the large number of prisoners. The fireplaces were broken which could pose great danger to those cooking as shown in plate 4.5 (h). However, the kitchens were fairly clean.

(a)

(b)

Plate 4.5. Kitchen roofs, '*jikos*' and fireplaces in prisons, 2009

Source: Researcher's own compilation, 2009.

Selection of Persons to Cook and Serve Food

There was need to find out the mode of selection of persons who prepare and serve food as viewed by prisoners. The criteria included: bad, unfair, favouritism, corruption, commercial, reward-based and tribal. These modes of selection of cooks were ranked on a scale of 1 to 5.

1 - Always, 2 -Very Often, 3 -Often, 4 - Rarely and 5 - Never.
The rankings of the various modes of selection as obtained from the respondents were averaged for each respondent and a general rank of the modes obtained. The general ranks were inclusive of all the modes of selection mentioned above.

The general mode of selection of persons to cook and serve was viewed to be *always bad, unfair, favouritism, corrupt, commercial, reward-based and tribal* by 8.8% of the total respondents. 31.5% of the respondents saw the mode of selection as being *very often* bad, unfair, favouritism, corrupt, commercial, reward-based and tribal. A cumulative percentage of 40.3% saw the mode of selection as being *always* and *very often* in the seven aspects of selection criteria. 22.5% of the respondents felt that the mode of selection was *often bad*, 28.9% and 8.3% felt that the mode of selection was *rarely* and *never bad* respectively in the aspects of selection enumerated above.

The levels to which prisoners' of individual prisons viewed the mode of selection in all the seven aspects of selection can be obtained directly from figure 4.4 below.

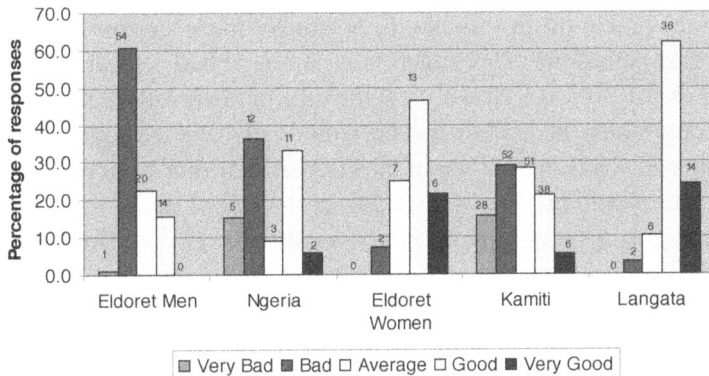

Figure 4.4. Selection of persons to cook and serve food in prisons, 2009.

Source: Researcher's own compilation, 2009.

Other Sub-Variables of Food Preparation

Cooking Equipment

Cooking equipment was rated as *very bad* and *bad* by 75.8% of the prisoners interviewed, which implied that the cooking equipment used in prison was poor. Observations of food preparation equipment in all prisons sampled except Langata Women's Prison were found to be in bad conditions. The cooking equipment used were water drums cut into halves and fitted with extra alluminium lining at the bottom to sustain heat as per plate 4.6 (a & b) . The drums were rusty and had no lids instead gunny bags were used to cover cooked food which when removed left pieces of string from the sack hence, food was cooked uncovered. Most of the drums were old, worn out and dirty at the time of observation. At the time of data collection, most of the cooking equipment in Langata Prison had holes such that water poured into the fire in the process of cooking resulting in a lot of smoke in the kitchen to the point that those cooking abandoned food on the fire to take a gasp of fresh air outside. In a bid to try and seal the holes, the prisoners placed flour on them and had to quicken the cooking of *ugali* by adding a lot of flour in order to beat the smoke and in the process the firewood got more wet and increased smoke emissions. This situation could have had a great effect on the quality of food. However, at the time of observations and taking photographs, the kitchen had been renovated and the equipment all changed. The current state of the kitchen and equipment in Langata Prison should be used as a model for the rest of the prisons. In the other prisons, the firewood used was dry enough. The fireplaces in Ngeria and Eldoret women were traditionally made with smeared mud and cow dung as per plate 4.6 (a & b). The cooking drums did not fit well on the fireplace such that a lot of direct heat and flames rose to the person cooking as shown in plate 4.6(a) whereas the flames went above the drums. The cooking sticks used were very heavy especially at the men's prisons which affected proper cooking of food as shown in plate 4.6 (e&f).

(a)

(b)

(c)

(d)

(e)

(f)

Plate 4.6. Cooking equipment in prisons, 2009

Source: Author's own compilation, 2009.

Cooking Ingredients

Observations by the researcher revealed that the cooking ingredients used were generally of low quality. Basic ingredients like tomatoes and onions were lacking. In most of the prisons, the flour used to cook *ugali* and porridge was fermented which resulted to a bitter and sour taste of food. The rice used was also of very low quality.

Method of Cooking

Method of cooking employed in prisons was boiling. Oil was poured into boiled vegetables that was full of water. In most of the prisons, unclean water was used to cook food whereby the process of cooking *ugali* involved boiling with 'not very clean' water then adding flour in very large quantities. The amount of *ugali* cooked was too large to get well cooked. In Kamiti Maximum, vegetables were cooked without washing and *magadi* soda was added to the vegetable to marsh them so that the watery liquid was served as vegetables. In Ngeria and Eldoret Women prisons, the vegetables were cut into large pieces while in Langata prison the vegetables were cooked without cutting. In Eldoret men's prison, salty water was served as vegetables. Conversations with prisoners in Eldoret men and Kamiti Maximum prisons revealed that vegetables were placed into a manila bag and dipped into hot water to get ready. Again water for cooking was sometimes used by warders and cooks to wash their faces before cooking.

Apart from Kamiti Maximum, all other prisons visited had running water in their taps. The water shortage in Kamiti Maximum was so bad such that on the first day of data collection, prisoners failed to have lunch. However, the management tried to ensure water was brought and lunch served as usual. However, most of the prisoners complained that they frequently went without lunch and were served double portions for supper. Furthermore, some of them indicated that they kept half of their portions for the next day incase lunch was not served.

Time Food was Prepared

Time food was prepared was rated as *very bad* and *bad* by 59.2% of the respondents. Time food was prepared varied in all the prisons except Kamiti Maximum. In the prisons, lunch was prepared between 8.00-9.00am while supper was prepared between 11.00-11.30 am. However, it was only at Kamiti Maximum Prison where food was prepared a day before consumption. The researcher was not able to observe the preparation and service of breakfast because it was difficult to access the prisons before 9.00 am. However, conversations between the researcher and prisoners revealed that in Kamiti Maximum porridge for breakfast was prepared the previous day. While in Eldoret men's prison, porridge for breakfast was prepared at night. In Ngeria, Langata Women and Eldoret Women prisons, porridge for breakfast was prepared at 4.30am. Prisoners described the porridge served as very light, lumpy and very often undercooked and sugarless.

Food Service

The aspects under food service included the temperature of food, service persons, equipment used for service, methods of service, time of service, place of eating, hygiene conditions of the service area and the quantity of food served as shown in table 4.7. However, the researcher presented detailed descriptive results on quantity of food served, temperature of food, time of food service and sequence of service.

The Quality of Catering in Kenyan Prisons

Table 4.7. Food service in prisons, 2009.

Name of Variable	Very Bad		Bad		Average		Good		Very Good	
	Fq	%	Fq	%	Fq	%	Fq	%	Fq	%
General way food is served	76	19.6	161	41.6	78	20.2	66	17.1	6	1.6
Persons serving food	101	26.1	145	37.5	57	14.7	78	20.2	6	1.6
Place of eating food	103	26.6	147	38.0	67	17.3	62	16.0	8	2.1
Time food is served	73	18.9	155	40.1	85	22.0	58	15.0	16	4.1
Plates used	143	37.0	116	30.0	55	14.2	68	17.6	5	1.3
Mugs used	246	63.6	66	17.1	33	8.5	40	10.3	2	0.5
Equipment used for service	143	37.0	116	30.0	55	14.2	68	17.6	5	1.3
Quantity of food served	103	26.6	170	43.9	61	15.8	43	11.1	10	2.6
Temperature of food served	110	28.4	132	34.1	82	21.2	53	13.7	10	2.6
Hygiene of food service	128	33.1	123	31.8	65	16.8	64	16.5	7	1.8
Average	123	31.7	133	34.4	64	16.5	60	15.5	8	1.9

Source: Researcher's own compilation, 2009.

Majority of the respondents that is, 66.1% felt that all the aspects under food service were *bad* to *very bad*. 16.5% felt that it was *average*, 15.5% felt that it was *good* while 1.9% were of the opinion that it was *very good*. This information is summarized in the average section in table 4.7 above. This means that food service was very poor in prisons.

Quantity of Food Served

Prisoners views on quantity of food served to them were solicited. Out of the 387 prisoners interviewed for this study, 26.6% of them felt that the quantity of food served to them was *very insufficient*, 43.9% thought the quantity was *insufficient*, 15.8% were of the view that the quantity was *average*, 11.1% of them said the quantity of food served was *sufficient* and 2.6% felt the quantity was *very sufficient*. The indication derived was that the quantity of food served to prisoners is actually small. The percentage of those who said the quantity was *very insufficient* or *insufficient* amount to 70.5%.

Those who were of the opinion that the quantity is either *sufficient* or *very sufficient* had a total percentage of 13.7%. The quantity of food in the prisons is thus said to be inadequate or poor. A summary of prisoner's views of quantity of food served in various prisons is shown in figure 4.5 below.

Figure 4.5. Views of quantity of food served in prisons, 2009.

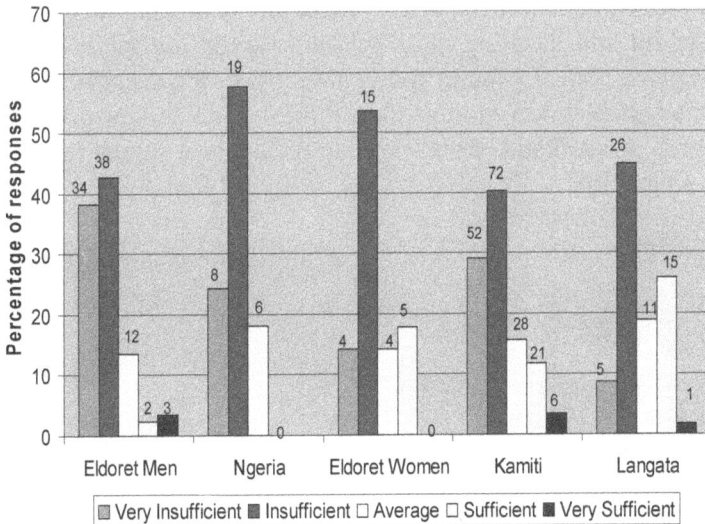

Source: Researcher's own compilation, 2009

Further from figure 4.5 above, in the individual prisons, a large percentage of those who felt the quantity of food was *very insufficient* came from Eldoret men with 38.2%, followed by Kamiti Maximum 29.1%, Ngeria 24.2%, Eldoret women 14.3% and Langata

8.6%. The response of *very insufficient* was most observed in Eldoret men prison.

Percentages for the other categories are as in figure 4.5 above. Worthy to note was the fact that Ngeria prison recorded 0% in the quantity of food in both the *sufficient* and *very sufficient* categories while respondents in Eldoret women also recorded 0% in the *very sufficient* category.

The researcher observed that the quantity of food served was too little compared to the work some of the prisoners did. Worth noting was the fact that women prisons served equal quantities of food to all prisoners irrespective of the individual status for example, pregnant and lactating mothers were served the same as other prisoners. Plate 4.7 (a&b) shows a sample of the quantity of *ugali* and vegetables served in prisons. Plate 4.7 (c&d) shows a double portion of *ugali* and beans served to prisoners at supper time after missing lunch.

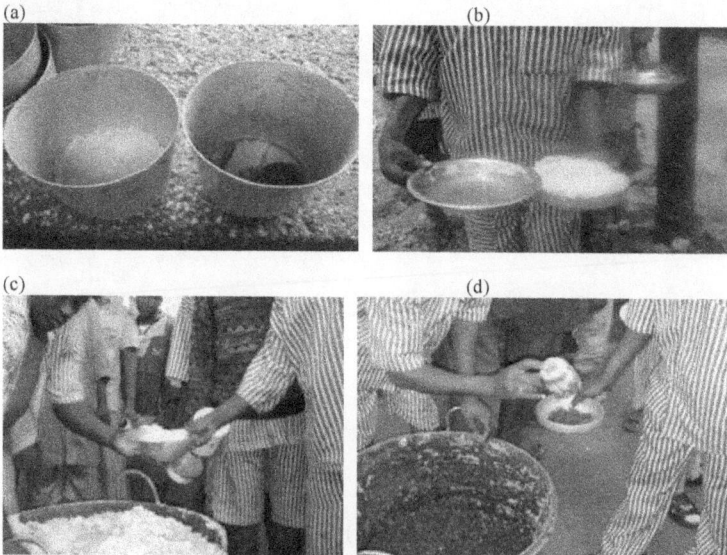

Plate 4.7. Quantity of food served in prisons, 2009.

Source: Researcher's own compilation, 2009

Further observations made by the researcher revealed that many prisoners, especially in Eldoret Men and Kamiti Maximum Prisons, kept urging the prisoners serving to add them more food. In addition, no food remained on plates which was another indicator of insufficient food, especially in Ngeria and Eldoret women prisons. However, in Kamiti Maximum and Eldoret Men's Prisons, the quantity of food served was not fairly and equally served to the point that some prisoners were served more food than others. However, the quantities served seemed to match the amounts stipulated in the Prisons Act. It was notable that food served to condemned prisoners was much more than that of ordinary prisoners.

Conversations between the researcher and prisoners revealed that prisoners could get more or less food than the normal portion by bribing cooks for about Kshs. 20-100. Money was used primarily to get better and more food from the kitchen in the evenings. For Sh50 or Sh100, one got a good quantity of better quality food smuggled out from the kitchen by the prisoners who worked there.

Further, it was intimated that sometimes an increased quantity of food was made available but the appearance, colour, taste, texture and smell of food deterred prisoners from eating. It was also reported that in Kamiti Maximum and Eldoret men's prison, sometimes food remained for the reasons stated and then taken to feed pigs by prison warders.

Temperature of Food Served

As far as the temperature of food served in prison was concerned, 28.4% of the total respondents felt that the temperature of food served was *very cold,* 34.1% felt the temperature of food served to them was *cold*, 21.2% were of the opinion that the temperature was *warm*, 13.7% felt it was *hot* and only 2.6% viewed the temperature of food served to be *very hot* as shown in table 4.8. The summation of *'cold'* and *'very cold'* gave a total percentage of 62.5% which suggested that the temperature of food in all the prisons was generally cold. Proportions of responses within the respective prisons are as shown in table 4.8 on the temperature of food served.

Table 4.8. Temperature of food served in prisons, 2009.

Prisons Name	Temperature of food served in prison										TOTAL
	Very Cold		Cold		Warm		Hot		Very Hot		
	No.	%	No.	%	No.	%	No.	%	No.	%	
Eldoret Men	18	20.2	25	28	21	23.6	17	19.1	8	9.0	89
Ngeria	17	51.5	9	27	6	18.2	1	3.0	0	0	33
Eldoret Women	14	50.0	9	32	2	7.1	3	10.7	0	0	28
Kamiti	41	22.9	61	34	45	25.1	30	16.8	2	1.1	179
Langata	20	34.5	28	48	8	13.8	2	3.4	0	0.0	58
Total	110		132		82		53		10		387
Percentage	28.4		34.1		21.2		13.7		2.6		

Source: Researcher's own compilation, 2009

From table 4.8 above, it can be concluded that the temperature of food served was poor. In support of the views of the prisoners, the researcher observed and recorded the temperatures of food using a food thermometer at intervals and took the weight of a portion of food using a food scale as shown in plate 4.8. The temperatures found were recorded and are as shown in table 4.9.

From the observations, the temperature of food kept decreasing from the time food was ready to the time of serving as in table 4.9. The temperature of vegetables served in Eldoret women recorded 65°c at the beginning of serving. In all the prisons, the temperature of food after cooking was high but all except Eldoret men's prison dropped drastically at the point of service and continued to drop as service progressed. However, the *ugali* served in Eldoret men's prison was very hot but too soft and conversations with the prisoners revealed that they were not able to hold and eat the *ugali* because it was too soft hence; they left it to cool to make it 'holdable' before eating. Therefore, as much as food was hot at the point of serving in Eldoret men, the researcher was not able to take the temperature of food at the time of consumption because they consumed food at their sleeping blocks to which access was restricted. Plate 4.8 is an illustration of how the researcher obtained food temperatures in the sampled prisons.

Table 4.9. Temperature of food taken at intervals in prisons, 2009.

Frequency	Eldoret Men	Ngeria	Eldoret Women	Kamiti Maximum	Langata
After Cooking	70°C	66°C	65°C	77°C	74°C
Before Service	65°C	41°C	38°C	45°C	35°C
1st Service	65°C	41°C	28°C	42°C	30°C
Mid Service	60°C	39°C	24°C	38°C	28°C
End of service	56°C	35°C	22°C	32°C	24°C

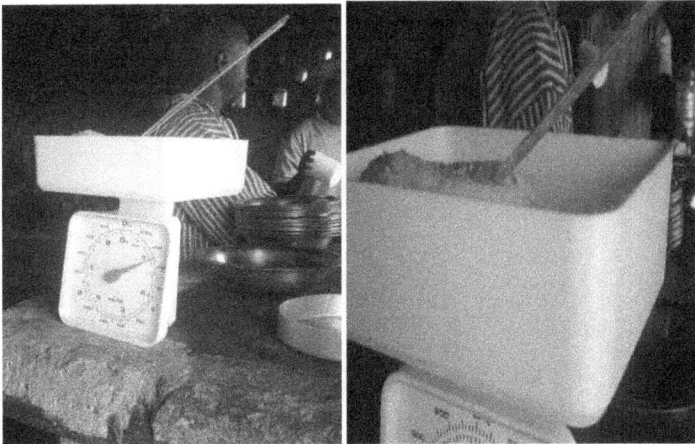

Plate 4.8. Measuring weight and temperature of food in prisons, 2009.

Source: Author's own compilation, 2009.

The researcher concluded that food served was cold for various reasons such as food prepared too early in advance, food service methods gave room for food to cool and lack of food warming mechanisms to retain the heat of food, after preparation, before, during and at the end of service.

Time of Service

In conducting this study, the researcher sought to establish the views of prisoners on the time food was served in prisons. In all the five prisons sampled, 18.9% of all the respondents said that the time of food service was *very early*, 40.1% said the time was *early*, 22% said the time was *average*, 15% felt the time was *good* and 4.1% said the time of food service in prison was *very good*.

Majority of prisoners were of the view that the time of food service was generally bad with a cumulative percentage of the *'early'* and *'very early'* categories totaling to 59% as compared to 19% which was a combination of the *'good'* and *'very good'* responses. Other percentages as relates to time of food service with respect to every prison are obtainable in figure 4.6.

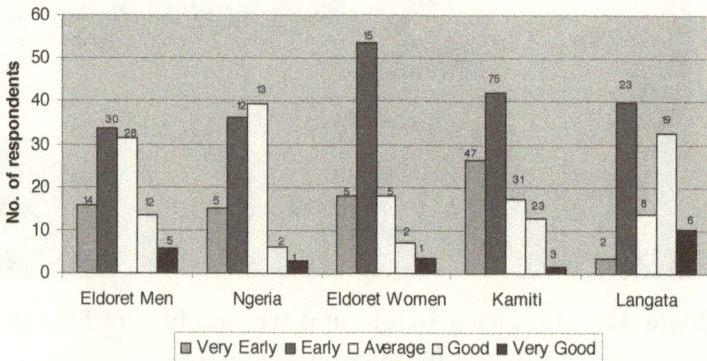

Figure 4.6. Time food is served in prisons, 2009.
Source: Researcher's own compilation, 2009

From the above figure, it was evident that many prisoners complained about the poor time of serving meals in prisons. Lunch was served at around 11.00 – 12.00 noon while supper was served at between 3.00 – 4.30pm. Prisoners felt their lunch and supper times were too early. Conversations with prisoners revealed that by the time they went to sleep, their stomachs were almost empty and thus had difficulty getting sleep.

General Views on the Method of Food Service

Of all the respondents interviewed, 61.2% felt that aspects of food service were 'very bad' and 'bad', 20.2% viewed it as 'average' while 18.7% viewed it as either "good" and 'very good". Observations were made on the way food was served in all the prisons sampled. When food was ready for service, it was removed from the cooking pans using a stick that was hooked onto the 'handles' of the pans before being lifted by the serving persons as shown on plate 4.9 (a&b).

(a)   (b)

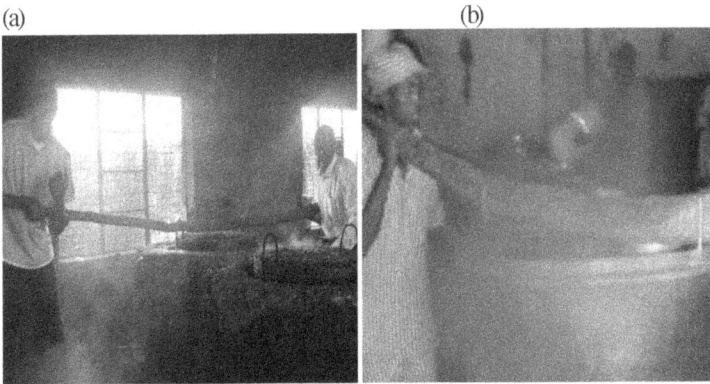

Plate 4.9. Transportation of food from kitchen in prisons, 2009.

Source: Author's own compilation, 2009.

The process of removing food from the cooking pans was very dangerous considering the amount of space available for the task. The persons removing the food must coordinate very well to avoid accidents. In Kamiti Maximum prison, the persons serving carried food to the different blocks that house prisoners using hand carts. In Langata, Ngeria and Eldoret women prisons, food was pre-served on plates before consumption.

Eldoret Women's Prisons Sequence of Food Service

In Eldoret women's prison, *ugali* was first apportioned for mothers and children as per plate 4.10 (a) then plates were placed on the floor as per plate 4.10 (b) and then *ugali* distributed into all the plates using bare hands as per plate 4.10 (c & d) followed by pieces of largely cut vegetables served on top of the *ugali* with a 'river of soup' poured on top of the food as per plate 4.10 (e). This food was then covered for about 45 minutes before being placed outside the kitchen on the pavement for prisoners to pick as per plate 4.10 (f).

(a)   (b)

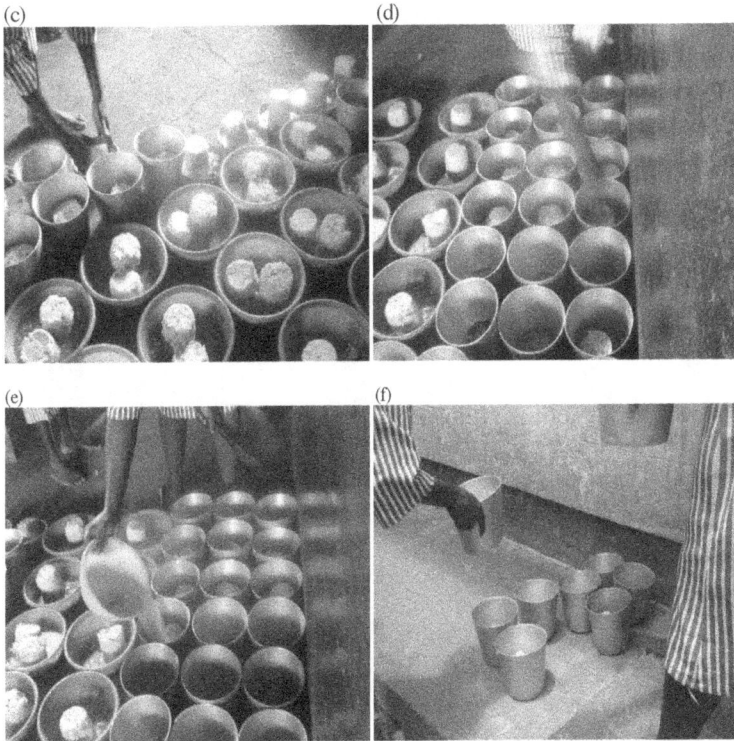

Plate 4.10. Food service sequence in Eldoret women's prison, 2009.

Source: Author's own compilation, 2009.

Ngeria Farm Prisons Sequence of Food Service

In Ngeria prison, *ugali* was apportioned in the kitchen one by one into all the plates and a depression created in the middle of each plate of *ugali* as per plate 4.11(a). All the plates were stacked together one on top of the other, regardless of the cleanliness of the bottom part of the plates and taken outside just before service as per plate 4.11(b). Later the prisoners were given each a plate of the *ugali* and queued for "vegetables" full of water as per plate 4.11(c). The depression on the *ugali* was meant to cater for the soup but instead during service, most of the prisoners removed the *ugali* and held it in their hands in order to be served soup into the bowl as shown in plate 4.11 (d).

(a)   (b)

c)   (d)

Plate 4.11. Food service sequence in Ngeria Farm prison, 2009.

Source: Author's own compilation, 2009.

Eldoret Men's Prisons Sequence of Food Service
In Eldoret men's prison, the person serving *ugali* dipped the serving container into a dirty yellow bucket of water to prevent it from

sticking as shown on plate 4.12 (a). The container used for serving was very dirty as per plate 4.12 (b). However, prisoners queued to be served first with *ugali* as per plate 4.12 (c) then the accompaniment which was salty water as shown in plate 4.12 (d). Food was served in an open air environment which subjected food to dust and other weather related effects. Conversations with prisoners in Eldoret men's prison revealed that if a prisoners' food fell down during service by mistake, he had to either pick up the food and eat or go hungry hence most of the time they chose the former which could lead to health related problems.

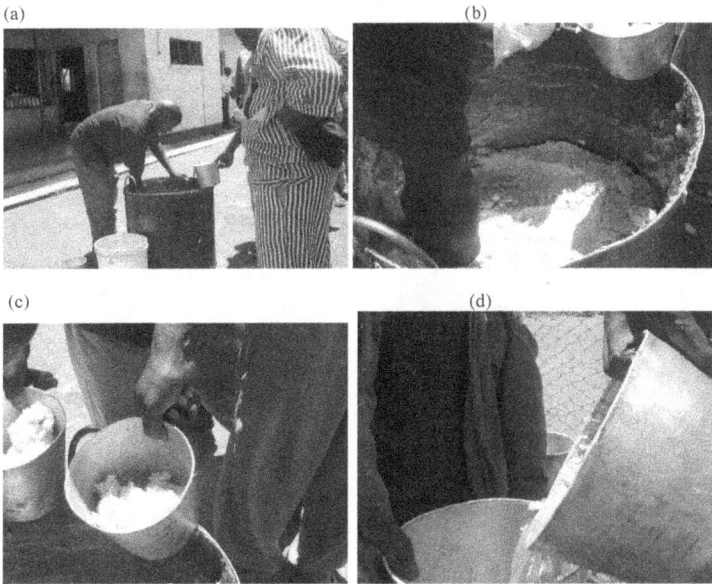

Plate 4.12. Food service sequence in Eldoret Men's Prison, 2009.

Source: Author's own compilation, 2009.

Kamiti Maximum Prison Sequence of Food Service

In Kamiti Maximum prison, food was divided in the kitchen according to each block and distributed by the service persons to each block for distribution. *Ugali* and beans were served into serving equipment as shown on plate 4.13(a) and carried to the blocks where food was served as shown on plate 4.13 (b) where prisoners prepare to carry beans. Once in the block, prisoners would queue first for *ugali*, followed by beans and finally a spoonful of vegetable oil as shown on plate 4.13 (c,d&e) respectively. Sick prisoners were served with green vegetables as shown on plate 4.3 (f). Because of insufficient plates, prisoners resorted to using plastic containers as shown in plate 4.3 (c,d&e).

(a)   (b)

 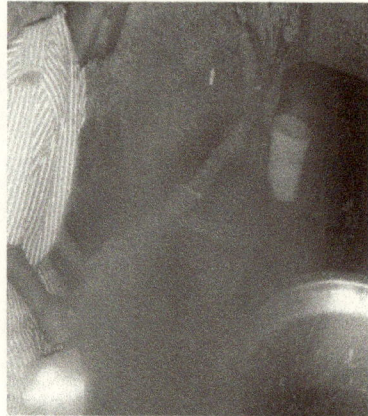

(e) (f)

Plate 4.13. Food service sequence in Kamiti Maximum Prison, 2009.

Source: Author's own compilation, 2009.

Langata Women's Prisons Sequence of Food Service

In Langata Women's Prison, food was pre-served in the kitchen before consumption. *Ugali* and vegetables were served in different plastic bowls and others on aluminium ones and stacked one on top of the other as shown on plate 4.14 (a&b). Since the food was served early, it was then covered with a pink cloth waiting for service time as shown on plate 4.14 (c). The food was placed on a cemented service counter. Prisoners queued outside the kitchen and picked plates of food one by one as shown on plate 4.14 (d).

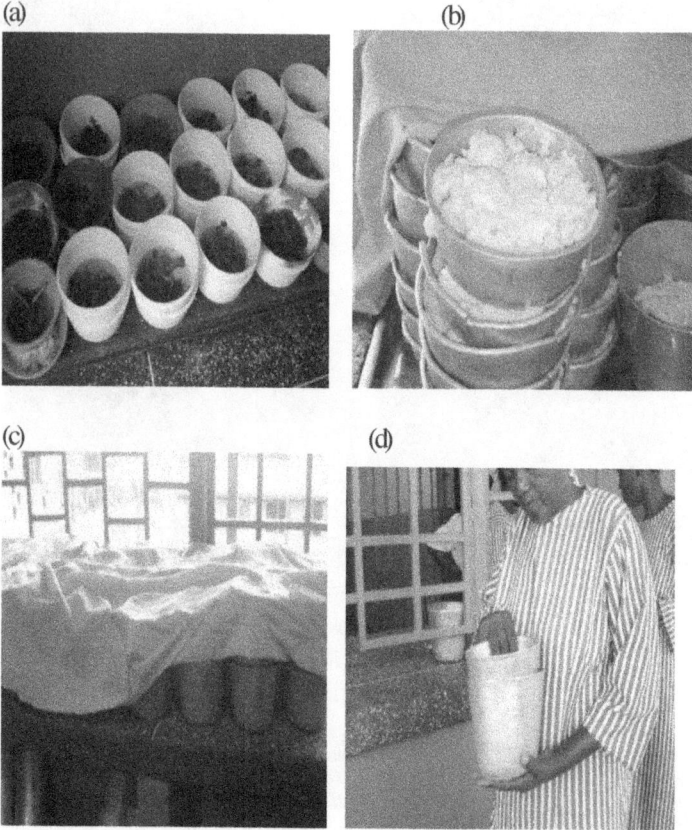

Plate 4.14. Food service sequence in Langata Women's Prison, 2009.

Source: Author's own compilation, 2009.

Service Equipment

In all the prisons except Langata Women's Prison, 20 litre plastic containers were used to serve vegetables which looked very unhygienic. Vegetable oil was served using a small fabricated spoon that looked like a nut as shown in plate 4.15 (a). In most prisons food was served using alluminium containers as shown in plate 4.15 (b) while others used plastic containers as shown in plate 4.15 (d). These serving containers and cups served as the measurement tool.

(a)

(b)

(c)

(d)

Plate 4.15. Food serving equipment used in prisons, 2009.

Source: Author's own compilation, 2009.

Place of Eating Food

The place for eating food was viewed as either *"very bad"* or *"bad"* by 64.6% of the respondents, 17.3% viewed it as average while 18.1% viewed it as either *"good"* or *"very good"*. Prisoners ate food in open air places which subjected the food to dust, rain, heat and other troubles of open air space dining as shown in plate 4.16 (a-d). Most of the prisoners did not wash their hands before eating and even if they washed, they touched the floors of where they were eating as they supported themselves when sitting on the floor to eat their food. In Eldoret Women's Prison, children ate the same food as their mothers and furthermore, they were served on the same plate hence, there was no separate menu for children as shown in plate 4.16 (e&f)

(a)   (b)

(c)

(d)

(e)

(f)

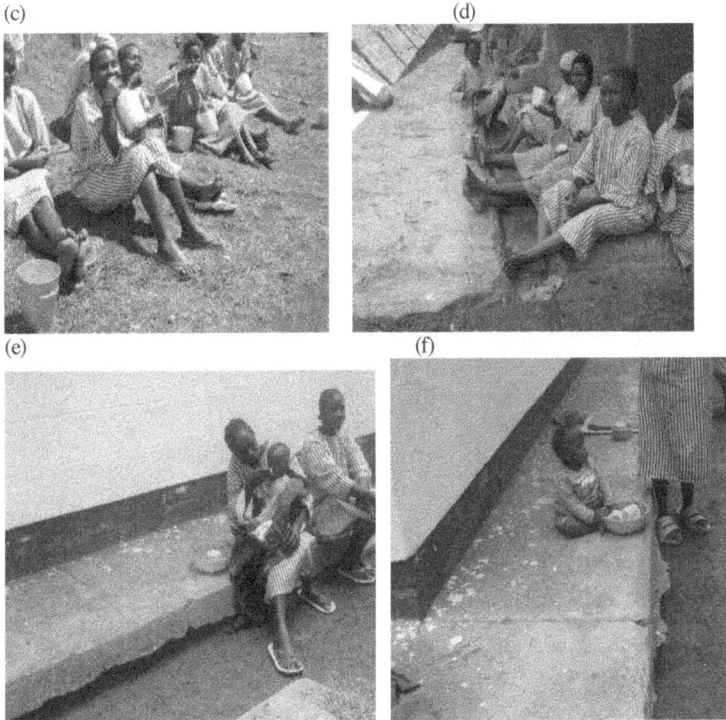

Plate 4.16. Place where food was eaten in prisons, 2009.

Source: Author's own compilation, 2009.

Plates Used for Eating

Plates used for eating in prisons were conically shaped and are referred to as *"mururus"*, which were made from aluminium as shown in plate 4.17 (a&b). The *'mururus'* serve as both plates and mugs. In all the prisons sampled, plates used were inadequate forcing prisoners to share plates or use plastic containers. In Langata and Eldoret Women Prisons, plastic plates were used to eat which could be very unhygienic if not well cleaned with hot water and detergents. Conversations between the researcher and prisoners revealed that in some of the prisons, two to three prisoners shared a plate such that all the portions of the prisoners sharing was put in the one '*mururu*' for example, porridge for three prisoners in one '*mururu*', meant that each drank the porridge in turns until it was finished which was very unhygienic. In one of the prisons visited, prisoners used plastic containers of '*kasuku, tily*" which they collected while working outside the prison. However, most of the '*mururus*' were old. The plates were washed in mass and most of them were not well cleaned as neither detergents nor hot water was provided as shown in plate 4.17 (c&d). Further conversations between the researcher and prisoners in Eldoret men prison revealed that the place used for washing utensils and bathing was the same.

Plate 4.17. *"Mururu"* and area for cleaning utensils in prisons, 2009

Source: Author's own compilation, 2009.

Storage

Observations by the researcher revealed that storage facilities were in a pathetic state.

Food Storage

The researcher visited the stores in all the prisons sampled for observation. In all the prisons visited, the stores were too old, food was stored together with non-food items e.g. maize, beans, vegetables, paint, fertilizer, wood, iron bars for building as shown in plate 4.18 (a&b). Vegetables and potatoes were stored on the floor as shown in plate 4.18(c&d). The floors and walls of all the stores sampled were rough with small potholes as shown in plate 4,18(e). All the stores visited were dark and poorly ventilated apart from the store in Langata Women Prisons. In all the prisons, the storage space was small and lacked storage facilities like fans, shelves, freezers apart from Eldoret Men's Prison which had a large store. The roofs of all the stores had holes which meant they leaked during rainy seasons which could affect the quality of food stored as shown in plate 4.18 (f). All the stores visited had indications of rodent infestations as most of the sacks containing maize and beans in the stores had been eaten by rats. In a nutshell, the storage facilities were pathetic.

Plate 4.18. Storage of food in prisons, 2009.

Source: Author's own compilation, 2009.

Water Storage

In Eldoret Women Prison, water was stored in cemented open sinks in the kitchen which did not guarantee hygiene and exposed the water to dirt that could lead to contamination as shown on plate

4.19 (a). Water tanks in Langata Women's Prisons were in good state but seemed inadequate incase of a water shortage as compared to the number of prisoners they hold. In Kamiti Maximum Prison, water shortage was acute but noteworthy was the fact that water handling practices in the prison exposed it to contamination and could easily lead to water borne diseases as shown on plate 4.19 (b). Drinking water was collected from the tanks.

(a)   (b)

Plate 4.19. Storage of water in prisons, 2009.
Source: Author's own compilation, 2009.

Overall View Level of Satisfaction with Catering Services in Prisons

The study established the level of satisfaction with the quality of catering in prisons from both the prisoners and the prison warders. This was of great importance as it allowed for comparison between prisoners response and that of prison warders on the same issue.

Of all the prison staff interviewed, 5.9% of them were *very dissatisfied* with the quality of catering in prison as shown on table 4.11 while 49.4% of the prisoners sampled were *very dissatisfied* with the quality of catering in prisons as shown on table 4.10. These two figures reveal a great difference in the level of satisfaction between the prison warders and the prisoners; with majority of prisoners being *very dissatisfied* and on the other hand only a few warders being *very dissatisfied*. This could in itself be an indicator that prison warders were comfortable with the current state of affairs as regards to catering. Table 4.11 shows that 14.5% of the 34 sampled prison warders said they were *dissatisfied* with the quality of catering in Kenyan Prisons. This compares to 40% of the prisoners who were *dissatisfied* with quality of catering as shown in table 4.10. Still, there was a marked difference in opinion between prison warders and prisoners on their levels of satisfaction. On adding the two categories of dissatisfaction; that is, *'dissatisfied'* and *'very dissatisfied'*, it was found that 20.6% of prison warders were generally *dissatisfied* as shown in table 4.11 as compared to 89.4% of prisoners who were generally *dissatisfied* as shown in table 4.10. The conclusion made was that prisoners were more dissatisfied as compared to prison warders.

Slightly satisfied with quality of catering services in prisons were 35.3% of the prison warders while the proportion of prisoners in this category was 8.5%. Here, it was realized that the proportion of prison warders went up while that of prisoners sharply went down. This just acted to demonstrate their differences in opinion about satisfaction with respect to catering in prisons; with prisons warders inherently in support of the state of affairs.

In the *'satisfied'* category, 38.2% of the prison staff said they were *satisfied* as shown on table 4.11. On the other hand, only 4.4% of prisoners said they were *satisfied* as shown on table 4.10. Again, the proportion of prison warders in this category went up further while that of prisoners went down further.

Table 4.10. Prisoners level of satisfaction with quality of catering in prisons, 2009.

Prisons Name	Prisoners level of satisfaction with quality of catering										TOTAL
	Very Dissatisfied		Dissatisfied		Slightly Satisfied		Satisfied		Very Satisfied		
	No.	%	No.	%	No.	%	No.	%	No.	%	
Eldoret Men	42	47.2	33	37.08	10	11.2	3	3.371	1	1.1	89
Ngeria	13	39.4	16	48.48	4	12.1	0	0.0	0	0	33
Eldoret Women	8	28.6	15	53.57	5	17.9	0	0.0	0	0	28
Kamiti	101	56.4	57	31.84	10	5.6	10	5.6	1	0.6	179
Langata	27	46.6	22	37.93	4	6.9	4	6.9	1	1.7	58
Total	191		143		33		17		3		387
Percentage	49.4		37.0		8.5		4.4		0.8		

Source: Researcher's own compilation, 2009

Of the 34 prison warders sampled, 5.9% of them were *very satisfied* with the quality of catering in prisons as shown in table 4.11 while only 0.008% of the prisoners were *very satisfied* as shown in table 4.10. On adding the two categories that imply general satisfaction that is, *'satisfied'* and *'very satisfied'*, it was realized that 44.1% of prisons warders were generally satisfied as shown in table 4.19 while only 4.408% of the prisoners were generally *satisfied* as shown in table 4.10.

Table 4.11. Warders level of satisfaction with quality of catering in prisons, 2009.

Prisons Name	Prison Warders level of satisfaction with quality of catering										TOTAL
	Very Dissatisfied		Dissatisfied		Slightly Satisfied		Satisfied		Very Satisfied		
	No.	%	No.	%	No.	%	No.	%	No.	%	
Eldoret Men	1	12.5	2	25	4	50.0	1	12.5	0	0.0	8
Ngeria	0	0.0	0	0	3	30.0	6	60.0	1	10	10
Eldoret Women	0	0.0	0	0	2	33.3	4	66.7	0	0	6
Kamiti	1	12.5	1	12.5	3	37.5	2	25.0	1	12.5	8
Langata	0	0.0	2	100	0	0.0	0	0.0	0	0.0	2
Total	2		5		12		13		2		34
Percentage	5.9		14.7		35.3		38.2		5.9		

Source: Researcher's own compilation, 2009

Throughout, it was realized that there were sharp differences in opinion of satisfaction between the prison staff and prisoners; while the prison warders were consistently in favour of the catering system, the prisoners were clearly against it.

With the focus now on satisfaction of prison warders alone within the sampled prisons, it was realized that only a small percentage of them were *dissatisfied* or *very dissatisfied* with some prisons polling 0% in these categories. In the *'very dissatisfied'* category in Eldoret men, Ngeria, Eldoret Women, Kamiti Maximum and Langata women's the percentages were 1%, 0%, 0%, 1% and 0% respectively. The percentages of *dissatisfied* prison warders were respectively, 2%, 0%, 0%, 1%, and 2% respectively. The proportion of the prison warders rose up sharply in the *'slightly satisfied'* and *'satisfied'* categories. Prison warders who were *slightly satisfied* were 50%, 30%, 33.3%, 37.5% and 0% respectively.

Those who were *satisfied* with quality of catering in prisons were 1% for Eldoret Men, 6% Ngeria, 4% Eldoret Women, 2%

Kamiti Maximum and 0% for Langata women. Lastly, in the *'very satisfied'* group, the percentages were 0%, 10%, 0%, 12.5% and 0% respectively.

In figure 4.7 below, are two pie charts graphically illustrating the percentage levels of satisfaction of catering by prisoners and prison warders respectively in the sampled prisons.

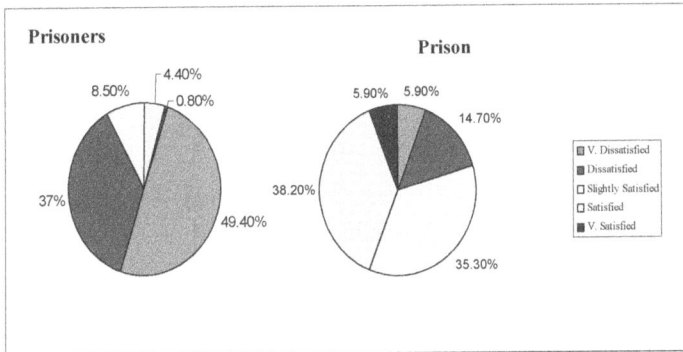

Figure 4.7. Percentage satisfaction of prisoners and prison warders with quality of catering in prisons, 2009

Source: Researcher's own compilation, 2009

Inferential Statistics

Inferential statistics deal with inferences about population based on results obtained from samples. In this study, multiple regression, independent samples t-test and ANOVA were used to analyse the data obtained from the field.

Multiple Regression

In this study, the dependent variable was quality of catering denoted as $\overline{Y}$. The dependent variable was made up of three sub-variables namely, general view of the level of satisfaction with the quality of the type of food in prison, the way food was cooked and the way food was served in prison. These three sub dependent variables were added and averaged to derive the dependent variable for this research ($\overline{Y_1}$)

The independent variables were type of food in prison ($\overline{X_1}$), food preparation ($\overline{X_2}$) and food service ($\overline{X_3}$). Each of these independent variables was made up of sub variables which were averaged to derive the main independent variables as follows;

For ($\overline{X_1}$), the sub independent variables averaged included:- taste of food, odour of food, texture of food, colour of food, nutritive value of food, appearance of food, food reduced as punishment, food increased for sexual favors, food used as inducement, food for sustenance and food used as punishment.

The sub independent variables that constitute the second independent variables ($\overline{X_2}$) included:- persons cooking food, conditions under which food was cooked, time food was prepared and selection of persons to prepare food in terms of bad, unfair, favoritism, corrupt, commercial, as reward and tribalism

Food service in prisons ($\overline{X_3}$) was derived by the average of the following sub independent variables included; quantity of food in prison, time food was served, place of eating food, plate used, mugs used, temperature of food in prison, persons serving food, general hygiene of food, provision of water and selection of persons to serve (bad, unfair, favoritism, corrupt, commercial, reward, tribalism).

Correlations

Correlation may be defined as the degree of relationship existing between two or more variables. The degree of relationship existing between two variables is called simple correlation. The degree of relationship connecting three or more variables is called multiple correlations (Koutsoyiannis, 1993).

A simple correlation was carried out to establish the degree of relationship between quality of catering in prison and the independent variables type of food, food preparation and food service and the following results obtained.

Table 4.12. Correlations in prisons, 2009.

	Quality	Type of Food	Food Preparation	Food Service
Quality	1.000			
Type of Food	0.661	1.000		
Food Preparation	0.544	0.521	1.000	
Food Service	0.640	0.589	0.523	1.000

Source: Author's own compilation, 2009.

From table 4.12, there exists a positive relationship between quality of catering and all the independent variables namely type of food, food preparation and food service.

The correlation coefficient between quality of catering in prisons and type of food was 0.661. The positive sign of the correlation indicates that the two variables tend to move together in the same direction, that is, they tend to increase or decrease together. The type of food had the highest level of relationship with the dependent variable with a correlation coefficient value of 0.661.

The correlation coefficient between quality of catering in prisons and food preparation was 0.544. The coefficient of correlation was positive and this is indicative of the fact that quality of catering services and food preparation move together in the same direction, increasing or decreasing together. Food preparation had the lowest level of relationship with quality of catering services in Kenyan prisons with a coefficient correlation figure of 0.544.

Lastly, the coefficient of correlation between quality of catering services in Prisons and food service stood at 0.640. With the positive coefficient, it was evident that the two variables (quality of catering services and food service) move together in the same direction. The degree of relationship was higher than that found between quality of catering services and food preparation but lower than that between quality of catering services and type of food.

All the three correlation coefficients were positive which was in agreement with the conceptual framework that hypothesizes that such aspects as type of food, food preparation and food service contribute positively to the ultimate quality of catering services in any given situation or institution under consideration.

A regression of (quality of catering in prison) against (type of food in prison), (food preparation in prison) and (food service in prison) was done and the results are summarized in tables 4.13 and 4.14 below.

Table 4.13. Coefficients

Coefficients (a)

Model	Unstandardized Coefficients		Standardized Coefficients	t	Sig.	95% Confidence Interval for B		Correlations			Collinearity Statistics	
	B	Std. Error	Beta			Lower	Upper	Zero Order	Partial	Part	Tolerance	VIF
1. (Constant)	-.175	.112		1.560	.120	-.395	.046					
Type of food	.480	.048	.426	9.938	.000	.385	.575	.661	.453	.343	.649	1.541
Food preparation	.204	.073	.252	2.798	.005	.061	.347	.544	.142	.097	.147	6.819
Food service	.684	.105	.622	6.53	.000	.478	.890	.640	.317	.226	.131	7.610

a Dependent Variable: Quality

Source: *Author's own compilation, 2009.*

Table 4.14: Model Summary

Model Summary

Model	R	R Square	Adjusted R Square	Std. Error of the Estimate	Change Statistics					Durbin-Watson
					R Square Change	F Change	df1	df2	Sig. F Change	
1	.737ᵃ	.543	.539	.5089	.543	151.637	3	383	.000	1.790

a. Predictors: (Constant), Food service, Type of food, Food preparation

b. Dependent Variable: Quality

Source: Author's own compilation, 2009.

The regression equation

$$= -0.175 + 0.480 + 0.204 + 0.684 + \mu_i$$

From the above model, we can note that there existed a positive relationship between quality of catering in prisons and all the three independent variables namely type of food, food preparation and food service based on the positive coefficients of the variables $B_1 = 0.480$ was the sample parameter estimate of the population parameter. It shows that when type of food changes by one unit percentage, quality of catering changes by 48%. It follows then that a unit increase in type of food in terms of taste, odour, texture, colour, appearance, nutritive value of food and purpose of food, will improve quality of catering services by 48% and vice versa.

The same argument was extended to the parameter estimate $\hat{B}_2 = 0.204$ linking quality of catering services and food preparation. The estimate tells us that when food preparation changes by a unit percentage the quality of catering services in the sampled prisons actually changes by 20.4%. Thus a one percent increase in the level of food preparation (persons cooking food, conditions under which food is cooked, time which food is prepared, cooking equipment and selection of persons to prepare food) will generate a 20.4% increase in the quality of catering services in the sampled prisons and vice versa.

Lastly, $\hat{B}_3 = 0.684$ was the sample parameter estimate of the true parameter. From the figure, we can deduce that a one percentage change in food service would bring about 68.4% changes in quality of catering in the sampled prisons. Indeed, a unit increase in food service would encompass all the sub variables that make it up including quantity of food served, time food was served, place of eating food, plates used, mugs used, temperature of food in prison, persons serving food, general hygiene of food service areas, provision of water and selection of persons to serve food.

Because the sample of prisons and prisoners selected by the researcher for this study was assumed to be representative of the population of prisons and prisoners, the deductions made above would surely apply to all the prisons in Kenya.

The deductions just above about the positivity of the parameter estimates are further supported by the results of the partial correlation coefficients. Partial correlation coefficient is by definition; "The measure of strength of the relationship between the criterion or dependent variable and a single predictor variable when the effects of the other predictor variables in the model are held constant" (Johnson and Bhattacharyya, 1987). Partial correlation coefficient is used to identify the independent variable with the greatest incremental predictive power beyond the predictor variables already in the regression model. The results of the partial correlation coefficient for this study are summarized as below;

$$rYX_1.X_2X_3 = 0.453$$
$$rYX_2.X_1X_3 = 0.142$$
$$rYX_3.X_1X_2 = 0.317$$

The figures show that type of food was the most important determinant of quality of catering in Kenyan Prisons. This is evident by the large partial correlation coefficient between the two variables; $rYX_1.X_2X_3 = 0.453$. Type of food was closely followed in importance by food service in the determination of quality of catering with partial correlation coefficient of $rYX_3.X_1X_2 = 0.317$. Of the three independent variables, food preparation ranked lowest in determination of quality of catering services in Kenyan prisons with a partial correlation coefficient of $rYX_2.X_1X_3 = 0.142$. It can then be concluded that ($\overline{X_1}$) was the most important determinant of

($\overline{Y}$) followed by ($\overline{X_3}$) and ($\overline{X_2}$). To improve quality of catering services therefore, more emphasis should be put on improving type of food, followed by food service and finally food preparation.

T-Tests (Tests of Research Hypothesis)

In order to test the three stated hypothesis, statistical significance of parameter estimates were established and thus enabling the researcher to establish the significance of the variables in the model and therefore their relative importance in determining the dependent variable.

The 95% confidence interval for the estimation of B_1 ranged between 0.385 and 0.575 for the lower and upper bound respectively. The true population parameter would lie in this range on 95 occasions out of 100 occasions this parameter was estimated. The standard error of the estimate stood at 0.048. This was a small value which implied more reliable prediction of $\hat{B}_1$. It is the estimate of how much the regression coefficient will vary between samples of the same size taken from the same population; that is, if one was to take multiple samples of the same size from the same population and use them to calculate the regression equation, this would be an estimate of how much the regression coefficient would vary from sample to sample.

The sample estimate $\hat{B}_1 = 0.480$ was found to be statistically significant at 1% level with 383 degrees of freedom with t=9.938 against critical t = 2.326. Clearly, type of food is a significant determinant of quality of catering services in Kenyan prisons. Since the two variables relate positively, then to improve quality of catering services in Kenyan prisons, the type of food must be improved. In essence, all the sub-variables making up type of food need to be improved that is, nutritive value of food, the sensory characteristics of food and the purpose of food in prisons.

With this result, we accept the hypothesis that the type of food served in prisons affects quality of catering in prisons since the calculated t=9.938 was greater than the critical t=2.326.

$\hat{B}_2$ which was the coefficient that relates quality of catering to food preparation stood at 0.204. The 95% confidence interval for the estimation of the parameter ranged between -0.061 to 0.347 for the lower and upper bounds respectively. The standard error of the estimates, S= 0.073, was also relatively small pointing to more reliable estimation of $\hat{B}_2$.

Food preparation was found to be statistically significant at 1% level with 383 degrees of freedom with t-statistic = 2.798 against critical t = 2.326. This showed that food preparation (X_2) was an important variable in the determination of quality of catering in prisons. The positive coefficient of X_2 was indicative of a positive relationship between food preparation and quality of catering in prisons. The implication here was that to improve quality of catering in Kenyan prisons, the level of food preparation had to be improved. An improvement in food preparation would be brought about by an improvement in all the sub-variables that constituted it namely, equipment used for cooking, the persons cooking food, the methods of food preparation and the time food was prepared.

With this result, we accept the hypothesis that food preparation in prisons affects quality of catering in prisons since the calculated t=2.798 was greater than the critical t=2.326.

B_3 was the coefficient that linked quality of catering services in the sampled prisons to food service in the sampled prisons. The 95% confidence interval for the estimation of this coefficient lied between 0.478 for the lower bound and 0.890 for the upper bound. The standard error for the estimate was S= 0.105. This figure was slightly higher than the previous two standard errors but was still good enough to ensure the significance of food service at a much lower percentage of 1%. Therefore the prediction was still reliable.

Food service was found to be statistically significant at 1% level of significance with (n-k) (387-4) degrees of freedom with t=6.530 against critical t = 2.326. Again food service in prison was a significant determinant of quality of catering services in prisons.

Because $\overline{y}$ and $\overline{x}$ were positively related, then to improve, has to be improved $\overline{y}$, $\overline{X_3}$. Since $\overline{X_3}$ was made up of several sub variables, then the improvement should encompass all the sub-variables that constituted food service (X_3) which included quantity of food served, the time food was served, the temperature of food served, the persons serving food, the conditions under which food was served, the place of eating, the equipment used for serving, the plates and mugs used to eat and the hygiene of food service.

With this result, we accept the hypothesis that food service in prisons affects quality of catering in prisons because the value of the calculated t=6.530 was greater than the critical t=2.326.

According to Koutsoyiannis (1993), the greater the value of t, the stronger was the evidence that $\hat{B}_2$ was significant. He went on to note that for a number of degrees of freedom greater than 8 the critical value of t (at 5% level of significance) for the rejection of the null hypothesis was two (2). The inference that can be made in light of the statements above with regard to this study was that type of food was a more important variable in explaining quality of catering in prisons, followed by food service and lastly food preparation.

Secondly is that we reject the null hypothesis that all regression coefficients are zero. The alternative hypothesis was accepted that the regression coefficients were significantly different from zero.

Since all the regression coefficients were found to be statistically significant, we can infer that the variables to which these coefficients relate type of food, food preparation and food service were all significant determinants of quality of catering services in the sampled prisons and by extension all prisons in Kenya.

R Square (R^2)

The coefficient of multiple determination (R^2) is by definition the proportion of total variation in the dependent variable (Y) explained by the multiple regression of say Y on X_1 and X_2 (Koutsoyiannis, 1993).

In this research, R^2 was found to be 0.543. From this figure of $R^2 = 0.543$, we can deduce that the multiple regression explains 54.3% of the variations in the dependent variable. More clearly, that type of food, food preparation and food service explains 54.3% of the total variations in quality of catering services in Kenyan prisons. With R^2 of 54.3% implies the model was significant in studying the situation in Kenyan prisons and that it captured the significant variables. The rest of the variations (100 − 54.3)% could be attributed to factors included in the error term.

Adjusted R^2 ($\bar{R}^2$)

The adjusted R^2($\bar{R}^2$) adjusts for the number of explanatory terms in a model. It increases only if the new term improves the model more than would be expected by chance. The adjusted R^2 can be negative, and will always be less than or equal to R^2.

The sample R^2 tends to optimistically estimate how well the model fits the population. The model usually does not fit the population as well as it fits the sample from which it is derived. Adjusted R^2 corrects R^2 to more closely reflect the goodness of fit of the model in the population. R^2 takes care of the fact that inclusion of more independent variables is likely to increase Regression Sum of Squares (RSS) for the same total sum of squares (TSS) and thus R^2 is made to increase. To take into account the reduction in degrees of freedom as additional explanatory variables are added, R^2 is computed (Koutsoyiannis, 1993).

Adjusted $R^2 = 0.539$. From this figure, we can infer that the multiple regression of quality of catering on the independent variables explains 53.9% of total variations in Y in the entire population of Kenyan prisons.

One-Way ANOVA

Analysis of variance is a data analysis procedure that is used to determine whether there are significant differences between two or more groups or samples at a selected probability level (Mugenda and Mugenda, 1999). ANOVA could be done one-way, two-way or more. One way analysis of variance which compares groups on one variable at different levels was used to test if there existed any significant differences among male and female prisoners and their perception of food preparation in Kenyan Prisons. In this study, ANOVA was used as it necessitates the comparison of two or more means. The results of the ANOVA are summarized in table 4.15 below;

Table 4.15 ANOVA results for food preparation in male and female prisons, 2009.

	Sum of Squares	Df	Mean Square	F	Sig.
Between Groups	76.924	1	76.924	107.894	.000
Within Groups	274.492	385	.713		
Total	351.416	386			

Source: Author's own compilation, 2009.

In table 4.15 above, the F-statistic, F=107.894 was found to be statistically significant at 1% level of significance with 1 and 385 degrees of freedom in the numerator and denominator respectively since it exceeded the tabulated value of F, . The null hypothesis that there are differences in food preparation in men and women prisons is rejected. We accept the alternative that food preparation is the same in men and women prisons in the sampled prisons and by extension all prisons in Kenya. Because food preparation was poor on average for all the sampled prisons, it was an indication that the situation applied to all the prisons, whether men or women prisons and that there were no particular differences in food preparation in either men or women prisons and by extension in all Kenyan prisons.

Independent Sample T-Test Results

Independent samples t-test is a test statistic used to establish if a sample mean from one group of cases differs significantly from another group of cases. Independent samples t-test differs from the normal t-student statistic that seeks to establish if a sample differs significantly from some arbitrary value as it assesses differences in means from two groups of cases.

According to Koutsoyiannis (1993), the t-test is appropriate if the variance of the parent population is unknown and the sample size is small such that (n<30). Secondly, t-test could be applied provided that the parent population is normal. For the application of t-statistic normality is crucial.

Since the population met the above criteria, a two tailed t-test was computed to test whether the actual food served in prison differed significantly from that stipulated in the Laws of Kenya, Prisons Act Cap 90 of the Kenyan constitution as shown in table 4.17. The assumptions made in the t-test computations are that:

a.   The population is normal
b.   Sample size is less than 30 (n<30)
c.   Variance is unknown
d.   The sample observations are random and in testing the equality of two means it was assumed that the population variances are the same

An independent samples t-test was computed to determine if there existed any significant differences between actual food served in prisons and the diet contained in the Prisons Act, Cap 90.

The foods used to carry out this test included maize meal, beans, soya flour, *Ndengu* (green grams), meat, milk, sugar, salt, vegetable oil (ghee), green vegetables, carrots, potatoes, sweet potatoes, spring onions, capsicum and tomatoes.

The frequency with which these foods were actually eaten in prison were ranked on a scale of one to five (1-5) *1 – Never eaten in prison, 2 – Rarely eaten in prison, 3 – Often eaten in prison, 4 – Very often eaten in prison, 5 – Always eaten in prison.* The averages of each 387 respondents for each food eaten was generated as shown on table 4.18 and compared with the food schedule in the Prisons Act Cap 90 as shown in table 4.17. The foods in the Prison's Act were ranked in the same manner.

The hypothesis were tested at 1% level of significance and the following results generated as shown on table 4.16 below.

Table 4.16. Independent samples t-test results comparing actual diet and Prisons Act diet, 2009.

	95% Confidence Interval of the Difference				
	Lower	Upper	t	df	Sig (2 tailed)
Actual diet in prison - Diet stipulated in Prison Act Cap 90	-2.27830	-0.72170	-4.108	15	0.001

Source: Author's own compilation, 2009.

The t statistic, t = -4.108 was found to be statistically significant at 1% level with 15 degrees of freedom since it was in excess of the tabular value of t=2.602. The null hypothesis that the meals actually served in prison was different from that stipulated in the prisons' Act Cap 90 is accepted and the alternative hypothesis is thus rejected. This result indicates that the frequency of meals actually served in prison significantly differs from the frequency of meals stipulated in the Prisons Act Cap 90. This in turn implied that the law regarding catering in prisons was not being implemented to the letter. Prisoners were not being served the meals at the stated frequencies in the Prisons Act and thus measures have to be put in place to ensure that they get the meals at the legislated frequencies. The fact that the frequency of food in prison differed from the frequency in the Act could itself be indicative of the poor nutritive value of food indicated by a number of prisoners interviewed for this study. A summary of foods included in the Prisons Act Cap 90 and the frequency of the food consumed in prisons are as shown in table 4.17. The tabulated frequency of food stipulated in the Prisons Act and the mean of the responses on a 5-point scale have been presented on table 4.19. The actual responses of the frequency of consumption of each of the food items in the Prisons Act Cap 90 are shown on table 4.18.

Table 4.17. Prisoners Diet (Monday to Sunday), Prisons Act Cap 90, 2008.

Diet	On each 4 days a week	On each 3 days a week
a)Carbohydrates/Vegetables Protein	Grams	Grams
Maize or other cereals	570	570
Beans	225	-
Soya flour	20	-
Green grams (*Ndengu*)	-	230
b) Animal Protein		
Fresh Meat	-	200
Dried skimmed milk	-	500 ml
Sugar	20	20
Salt	15	15
c) Fats		
Fortified vegetable oil or		
Fortified vegetable ghee	16	16
d) Fresh vegetables and fruit		
Green leafy vegetables	120	-
Carrots	-	90
Irish potatoes or sweet potatoes	30	115
Spring onions	30	30
Capsicum	30	30
Tomatoes	-	30

Source: *Laws of Kenya, Prisons Act, Cap 90, Section 74, first schedule, 2008.*

Table 4.18: Frequency of food items consumed by prisoners in prisons, 2009.

Name of food item	Frequency	Response	%age	Name of food item	Frequency	Response	%age
Maize Eating (Ugali & Porridge)	Always	380	98.2	Salt usage	Always	340	87.9
	Very Often	4	1.0		Very Often	18	4.7
	Often	2	0.5		Often	15	3.9
	Rarely	0	0.0		Rarely	2	0.5
	Never	1	0.3		Never	12	3.1
Beans eating	Always	369	95.3	Vegetable oil usage	Always	227	58.7
	Very Often	6	1.6		Very Often	39	10.1
	Often	3	0.8		Often	41	10.6
	Rarely	1	0.3		Rarely	48	12.4
	Never	8	2.1		Never	32	8.3
Soya flour eating	Always	2	0.5	Green vegetables eating	Always	225	58.1
	Very Often	0	0.0		Very Often	28	7.2
	Often	3	0.8		Often	57	14.7
	Rarely	9	2.3		Rarely	45	11.6
	Never	373	96.4		Never	32	8.3
Green grams (ndengu eating)	Always	1	0.3	Carrots usage	Always	1	0.3
	Very Often	0	0.0		Very Often	0	0.0
	Often	0	0.0		Often	2	0.5
	Rarely	1	0.3		Rarely	3	0.8
	Never	385	99.5		Never	381	98.4
Meat Eating	Always	0	0.0	Potatoes eating	Always	15	3.9
	Very Often	10	2.6		Very Often	8	2.1
	Often	299	77.3		Often	55	14.2
	Rarely	60	15.5		Rarely	177	45.7
	Never	18	4.7		Never	132	34.1
Milk drinking	Always	1	0.3	Sweet potatoes eating	Always	1	0.3
	Very Often	2	0.5		Very Often	1	0.3
	Often	12	3.1		Often	0	0.0
	Rarely	10	2.6		Rarely	7	1.8
	Never	362	93.5		Never	378	97.7
Sugar Usage	Always	90	23.3	Tomatoes, Onions & Capsicum	Always	0	0.0
	Very Often	18	4.7		Very Often	0	0.0
	Often	39	10.1		Often	0	0.0
	Rarely	92	23.8		Rarely	0	0.0
	Never	148	38.2		Never	387	100.0

Source: Author's own compilation, 2009.

Table 4.19. Tabulated frequency of food on a 5 point Likert scale in prisons, 2009

DIET	CAP 90	ACTUAL SERVED
Maize	5	5
Beans	4	5
Soya	4	1
Green Grams	3	1
Meat	3	3
Milk	3	1
Sugar	5	3
Salt	5	5
Vegetable Oil	5	4
Green Vegetables	4	4
Carrots	3	1
Irish Potatoes	5	2
Spring onions	5	1
Capsicum	5	1
Tomatoes	3	1

Source: Table 4.17 and 4.18, 2009.

CHAPTER FIVE

Discussion, Conclusions and Recommendations

This chapter presents discussions, conclusions and recommendations for the study. The purpose of this study was to investigate the factors affecting quality of catering in selected prisons in Kenya. It was inspired by the current calls for reforms in Kenyan prisons. The research was guided by four objectives that focused on areas considered key by the researcher in examining the quality of catering in Kenyan Prisons.

1.   First was to investigate the extent to which the type of food served to prisoners affects the quality of catering in prisons.
2.   Second, was to establish the extent to which food preparation affects the quality of catering in prisons.
3.   Third objective was to establish how food service affects the quality of catering in prisons.
4.   Finally, the fourth objective sought to examine the extent to which the actual food served to prisoners differs from the menu items stipulated in the Prisons Act Cap 90. The researcher hypothesized that there was a relationship between quality of catering in prisons and the type of food, and the preparation and service of food in prisons. In addition, the researcher also hypothesized that the actual food served to prisoners differs from the menu items stipulated in the Prisons Act Cap 90.

Each of the three independent variables posted on the objectives correlated highly with the dependent variable quality of catering. These results showed an overall reality that quality of catering was affected by the type of food served, and the preparation and service of food in prisons. The regression analysis put into perspective the importance of the independent variables to the quality of catering in Kenyan prisons. The leading factor affecting the quality of catering was the type of food, followed by food service and, lastly, food preparation. The overall effect of all these combined was coefficient

of determination value of $R^2 = 0.543$ explaining 54.3% of the variance. This means that this study established that the type of food, food preparation and food service explained 54.3% of the total variations in quality of catering in Kenyan prisons. The rest of the variation 45.7% can be attributed to other factors included in the error term. As a result, this study accepts the hypothesis that type of food, preparation and service of food affect the quality of catering in Kenyan Prisons. All in all, the results led to acceptance of the three hypothesis that:

a)   Type of food affects the quality of catering in prisons
b)   Food preparation affects the quality of catering in prisons
c)   Food service affects the quality of catering in prisons

One-way ANOVA was used to test the difference among men and women prisons in their perception of food preparation in Kenyan Prisons. The F-statistic at 107.894 was found to be statistically significant at 1% level of significance with 1 and 385 degrees of freedom in the numerator and denominator respectively as it exceeded the tabular value of f(1,385)=6.63. The results indicated that there was no difference in food preparation between men and women prisons in Kenya.

The independent samples t-test was computed to test whether the actual food served in prison differs significantly from that stipulated in the Prisons Act Cap 90. The t-statistic of 4.108 was found to be statistically significant at 1% level with 15 degrees of freedom since it was more than the tabular value of t, t=2.602. The null hypothesis that the food served to prisoners differs from that stipulated in the Prisons Act Cap 90 was accepted. The results indicate that the food served to prisoners was different from that stipulated in the Prisons Act Cap 90. This implies that the law regarding catering in prisons was not being followed to the letter.

Objective One - Type of Food

Nutritive value of food was poor with 82.4% of prisoners viewing it as either *very bad* or *bad*. Observations by the researcher further supported the prisoner's position. This can have effect on prisoner's health and hence, hamper efforts of successful reforms. According to Bosworth, (2004), healthy prisoners, it was believed, would be productive workers and ultimately, reformed citizens. Hence good nutritive value could positively reinforce the behaviour of prisoners. McLellan referred to research which showed that giving young people healthier food could lead to improved behaviour. In addition, most prisoners ate a great deal of fat, sugar and sodium before imprisonment, and also very little fruit and vegetables hence it is possible that encouraging prisoners to eat nutritious food might be a contribution not only to healthier living but also to less destructive behaviour.

Research carried out by the National Audit Office, (1997) on 231 prisoners at Aylesbury Young Offenders Institution showed a statistically significant link between supplementing prisoners' diets with vitamins, minerals and fatty acids and fewer recorded incidents of anti-social behaviour. The research highlighted that anti-social behaviour decreased with good nutrition indicating the importance of providing prisoners with meals containing the recommended levels of nutrients.

This study found that the sensory characteristic of food in terms of colour, taste, odour, appearance and texture were all poor. Out of 387 prisoners, 320 prisoners which accounts for 82.6% percent of the respondents rated the sensory characteristic of food as either *very bad* or *bad*. Observations by the researcher found that the colour of food was pale, the taste was bitter, the appearance was very unappetizing and the texture very bad. According to Sydow and Rolfe (1980), aesthetic value especially flavour is very important for food choice and food consumption, making it also important from the nutritional point of view: a nutritious food with bad aesthetic properties will never or rarely be consumed and even if it is consumed, digestion will be negatively affected.

Food in Kenyan prisons serves as a tool of punishment through the penal diet as stipulated in the Prisons Act Cap 90. This is definitely negative reinforcement which could hamper the reform of prisoners. According to Burton, *et al*. (1998), other than restricting access to the commissary, food may not, by law, officially be used as punishment. Further Burton, et al. (1998) stated that inmates, even when in disciplinary segregation, are entitled to nutritionally adequate meals, ordinarily from the menu of the day for the institution. Food was found to be used for sexual favours especially by cooks in the male prisons. 57.3% of the respondents interviewed revealed that food was *always* or *very often* used for sexual purposes. In the study, type of food was found to be a significant determinant of quality of catering in prisons that led to the acceptance of the hypothesis that indeed type of food affects quality of catering in Kenyan prisons.

Objective Two - Food Preparation

Food preparation in Kenyan prisons was found to be poor as 67.1% of the respondents rated it as either *"very bad"* or *"bad."* The predominant method of food preparation in all the prisons was boiling. Proper preparation of food is more than merely boiling. The boiling was often done to extreme levels whereby important nutrients got lost, the taste was distorted, the colour and appearance changed and proper texture of food were affected. The persons preparing food were not trained and so did not adhere to common standards of preparing food. 61.8% of the respondents rated the persons cooking food as *very bad* and *bad*. Furthermore, the conditions of food preparation were equally poor and could be summed up as being largely unhygienic. The hygiene of food preparation was rated as either *very bad* or *bad* by 69% of the prisoners interviewed.

The time food was prepared was bad and was rated as either *very early* or *early* by 59.2% of the respondents. Previous studies showed that food prepared too early allow for bacterial growth before serving and could cause food poisoning. Observations by the researcher witnessed food cooked a day earlier and in other situations food cooked much earlier than the service time. Special foods were not served in prisons, notwithstanding the prevailing conditions. For those who were sick, the quantity of food was increased. HIV prisoners sometimes received soya flour from Ampath. In Zimbabwe, pregnant or nursing mothers and persons who are ill and for whom a particular diet has been prescribed by a doctor, are allowed to receive visitors who bring food. According to Whitney, teenagers and young adults, women who are pregnant or lactating, and women past menopause are advised to have three servings of milk, and teenagers who are pregnant or breastfeeding should have four servings of milk.

The equipment used in food preparation was rated as either *very bad* or *bad* by 75.8% of the prisoners interviewed. Poor equipment affects the quality of food and also affects the outcome of the food in terms of colour, taste, flavour, appearance, smell and texture. Poor equipments also cause accidents in the kitchen and can also affect the health of those cooking. Observations by the researcher confirmed that the equipment used for cooking were in a very bad state in all the prisons sampled apart from Langata Women's Prison. The general way food was cooked was rated as either *very bad* or *bad* by a majority of 70% of prisoners interviewed. In total, the results obtained for this study showed that food preparation was significant in explaining quality of catering in Kenyan prisons and thus the postulation that food preparation affects quality of catering was confirmed.

Objective Three - Food Service

Time between lunch and supper was too close whereas the time between supper and breakfast was too long. Lunch was served between 11.00am – 12.00 noon while supper was served between 3.00pm – 4.30pm. This means a difference of about four hours between lunch and supper. Breakfast was served at 6.30am and supper at 3.00pm which means a difference of about 15½ hours. The times seem to be fixed in order to accommodate staff working patterns. According to Flynn, (1998), this contravenes the Prison Service standard of a maximum of 14 hours between evening meals and breakfast. According to National Audit Report, (1997), prisoners should not go longer than 14 hours between meals and that if the gap between the evening meal and breakfast exceeds 14 hours and prisoners are locked up in the evening, the catering standards require that they should be provided with an additional snack.

Time food was served was too early and too far from the time food was prepared. 59% of prisoners interviewed felt that the time food was served was either *very early* or *early*. According to the National Audit Office (2006), food often not served within 45 minutes of its preparation risks losing some of its palatability, nutritional content and could cause deterioration in the nutritional profile of food. The quantity of food served was inadequate with a total of 273 out of 387 prisoners indicating that it was either *very insufficient* or *insufficient* which accounted for 70.5% of the respondents. Observations by the researcher confirmed that the quantity was inadequate for normal adults. Previous studies indicate that food is of vital importance to human beings forced to do hard, wearing labour. It is understood, of course, that a prison is not a high-class hotel and that meals *de luxe* are not to be expected; but a ration that will sustain life and keep a prisoner in good physical condition is certainly necessary if any marked success is to be achieved in making the criminal a law-abiding citizen.

O'Hare (2006), states that the most galling bitterness, the most corroding and socially dangerous sense of injustice, is bred in the soul of a hungry convict by the fact that he knows he is performing forced labour whose value is far beyond the cost of his maintenance, and that even the insufficient sum appropriated for his food is misused, or stolen, and he is robbed of his hard earned and lawful ration. She further states that, prisons will never be able to reform hungry convicts. In fact, it is impossible to find decent, socially-minded people anywhere whose stomachs are clamouring for food. No male or female, for that matter is really civilized when hungry. The only way to live in approximate comfort with the human being is to feed them.

Temperature of food served in all the sampled prisons except for Eldoret Men's Prisons was cold. 62.5% of the prisoners interviewed rated the temperature of food served as either *very cold* or *cold*. Actual measurement of temperatures of food by the researcher confirmed that in most of the prisons sampled, food was served cold. Previous studies have shown that cold food destroys the necessary nutrients and cause diseases. All the conditions of service were found to be unhygienic. This included the equipment used, the persons serving food, the place where food was served and eaten and the state of the plates used for eating food were all found to be very unhygienic. The equipment used for service was rated as either *very bad* or *bad* by 67% of the prisoners interviewed. 63.6% rated the persons serving food as either *very bad* or *bad*, 64.6% rated the place of eating as either *very bad* or *bad* while 67% rated the plates used as either *very bad* or *bad*. There were no mugs used in all the prisons but the *"mururu"* served as both plates and mugs.

The place of eating was rated as either *"very bad"* or *"bad"* by 64.4% of the respondents. There were no dining halls in all the prisons sampled hence meals were eaten in open air grounds. This condition subjected food to effects of weather such as dust, wind, rain and all other weather forces. This can further expose food to contamination. The general view of the way food was served in prisons was rated as either *very bad* or *bad* by 61.2% of the prisoners interviewed. However, the statistical test results led to acceptance of research hypothesis that food service affects the quality of catering in Kenyan prisons.

Objective Four – Menu Items

The frequency of menu items served to prisoners sharply differed from the menu items contained in the Prisons Act Cap 90. The Prisons Act Cap 90 of the Kenyan constitution was formulated to ensure that proper type of food was provided to prisoners. Often factors like nutrition and quantity of ration were also factored in the formulation of the Act.   The implication of the Act faces challenges in terms of:

  i.   Limited prison's budget
  ii. Corruption between warders and cooks and also the prison administration in general
  iii. Unscrupulous contractors who supply sub-standard food items
  iv. Large number of prisoners to attend to.

Storage

Storage facilities in all the sampled prisons were in a pathetic state. In theory, proper storage of food is very important for the following reasons: preservation of the important nutrients in the food; to ensure constant supply of food all the time in order to avoid shortages.

The two objectives above were not being met because of the following reasons observed in all the prisons:

  i.   Lack of proper ventilation and lighting in the stores;
  ii. Lack of storage equipment like shelves, cool areas, fridges;
  iii. Poor aeration due to lack of fans;
  iv. Old structures with rugged floors and leaking roofs; and
  v.   Untrained storekeepers who lack basic knowledge in stores management.

Water storage facilities were inadequate and not well maintained which could easily lead to water borne diseases such as cholera. Storage of water in open sinks used for cooking, lack of treated or boiled drinking water could also lead to water borne diseases.

Q-CAT MODEL (Quality of Catering Model)

The research findings of the study and the positive results of the hypotheses tested indicate that all variables (Type of food, food service and food preparation) affect the quality of catering in Prisons. In addition, observations indicated that storage was also critical in maintaining quality of catering. Apart from prisons, the results can be reflective of other catering institutions.

Consequently, the researcher proposes a model (adopted from the conceptual framework of the study) that depicts the results to be referred to as the Q-CAT MODEL (Quality of Catering Model). This is illustrated using the following diagram.

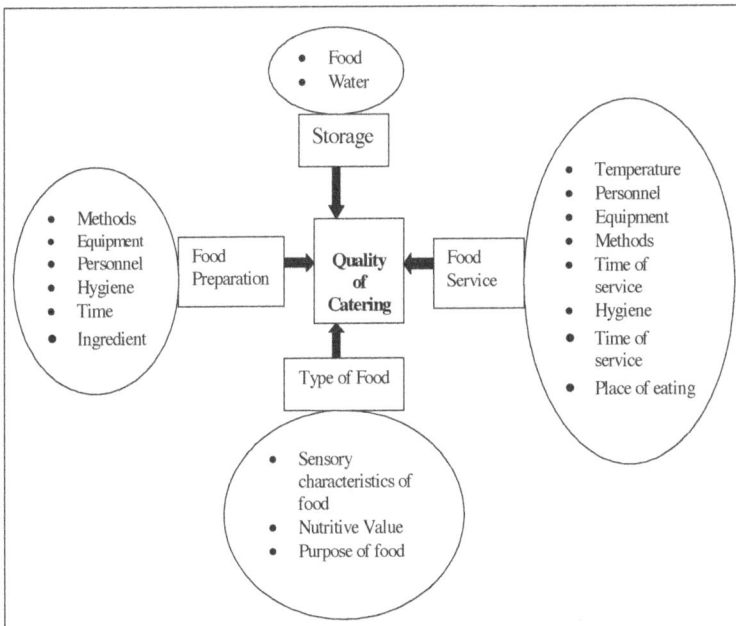

Figure 5.1: Proposed Model for Quality of Catering

Conclusions

From this study, conclusions can be drawn based on the independent variables, type of food, food preparation and food service and their effect on the dependent variable, quality of catering. Firstly, the type of food served to prisoners in Kenyan prisons is bad and affects the quality of catering. This conclusion has been drawn by the fact that the nutritive value of food was below expected levels and does not contain all the required nutrients. Porridge was served without sugar; salty water was served as vegetables; vegetable oil was served separately from the vegetables; pieces of meat served was too little to give adequate protein; and, the required vitamins in the food seemed to lack.

Furthermore, the sensory characteristic of food in terms of colour, taste, appearance, odour and texture of food were poor. The taste of *ugali* was bitter and the appearance had a pale look. The texture of *ugali* in some prisons was either too soft or to dry. In another prison they cooked *ugali* a day or two before consumption making it taste stale and too hard to serve and worse still, too cold to eat. The vegetables served were mashed and looked like porridge and in other prisons they were poorly cut and presented. The purpose of food in prison has resulted into perpetrating bad behaviour such as homosexuality, corruption and bribery. It was found that in most of the male prisons, food was used for sexual favours and also used for trade. Prisoners who made mistakes were punished by receiving the penal diet of half ration as stipulated in the Prisons Act.

Secondly, food preparation areas and the persons cooking maintain poor hygiene. Furthermore, the equipment used for cooking was of poor quality. The cooking equipment and the kitchen generally posed a great risk to the health of prisoners. The cooking equipment were old and worn out. The kitchens were poorly ventilated and the roofs had holes that leaked during rainy seasons. The methods of cooking used destroyed vital nutrients in food because it was boiled in too much water and for long hours. The time food was prepared was also too early to the extent that food nutrients were destroyed. Cooks were the chief perpetrators of homosexuality. They used food to entice the culprits by increasing or drastically decreasing their serving portions to make them desperate and succumb to the vice. There was a lot of business in the kitchens both with the cooks and prison warders. Selling food was the order of the day in prison kitchens. Prisoners who can afford to buy food take full advantage hence really enjoy as food was sold for about Kshs. 5 – 100. To get an extra piece of meat, prisoners paid Kshs. 5. The ingredients used for food preparation were of poor and low quality. No special diets were prepared for any medical conditions or religious purposes.

Thirdly, food service in prison was very poor and affected the quality of catering. The equipment used to serve food was of poor quality and very unhygienic. The prisoners who serve food were not hygiene conscious and the place where food was served from was very unhygienic. Food was sometimes served using bare hands which could result in the spread of diseases. Most of the prisons served food from open air spaces that attracted a lot of dust which could destroy the nutritive value of food. The time food was served was too early especially lunch and supper. There were no designated places for prisoners to eat hence; the environment in which food was eaten was very unhygienic. The temperature of food at the time of service was very cold apart from Eldoret Men's prison. This was mainly due to the early preparation of food and keeping food for long periods before eating time. The plates used for eating were inadequate to the point that some prisoners had to share their plates or wait until others had eaten. The cleaning of plates was done under very unhygienic conditions and was done in a central place with no detergents or hot water. The quantity of food served to prisoners was too little compared to the work they did. Good and adequate water for washing hands need urgent attention to reduce water borne related diseases such as cholera.

Fourthly, the storage facilities were also in a pathetic state. All food and non-food items were all stored in the same room which could easily lead to contamination of food. The stores were not well ventilated and were infested with rodents that destroyed the quality of maize and other food ingredients. The floors and walls of the stores were in a pathetic state. The current state of the stores affect the quality of catering in prisons. In addition, the menu items stipulated in the Prisons Act Cap 90 are not adhered to in practice. Most of the items were never provided in the prisons.

Finally, based on the above position of the independent variables, it can be concluded that the quality of catering in Kenyan prisons is poor and to a great extent it is caused by the type of food served to prisoners, the way food is prepared and the way it is served. Further, other factors including the storage facilities and the amount of funds allocated to the prisons affect the quality of catering in Kenyan prisons. Therefore, there is need to improve the type of food served in prisons, the way it is prepared and the way it is served in order to enhance the quality of catering in prisons. Improvement of the quality of food can improve the self esteem of the prisoners by valuing their dignity and in turn the prisoners may feel appreciated as human beings and hence, reform.

Recommendations
The researcher recommended the following:

Prisons Act Cap 90
- The menu items stipulated in the Kenya Prisons Act, Cap 90 section 74 under 'first schedule' should be adhered to. This means *ndengu*, milk, carrots, onions, tomatoes, capsicums, potatoes and sweet potatoes should be purchased and provided in all the prisons.
- Incorporate a diet for children born in prisons or those accompanying their mothers. Fruits should be incorporated into the menu at least once or twice a week.
- Varied scales of diets as food rations should be increased for prisoners on the basis of their labouring capacity such that the quantity of food should be more for those who work in the industry, pregnant and lactating prisoners. In addition, the quantity for young prisoners should be increased so that they are not tempted to engage in homosexuality.

- The penal diet should be scraped as food should not be used as punishment as it negatively reinforces behaviour of prisoners.

Type of Food
- Increase animal protein, fats and vitamins in the diet
- Introduce slight variation in the diet

Food Preparation
- Kitchens should be renovated and fitted with modern equipment to cater for mass production. In addition ventilation in the kitchen should be improved by having hoods above the cooking equipment plus chimneys to channel smoke outside the kitchen.
- The persons preparing and serving food should be provided with different clothes/uniforms to be used for cooking because most of the prisoners may be wearing their uniforms, sleeping in them and cooking in them.
- Kitchen personnel should undergo regular medical checks and be in possession of medical certificates to ensure healthy persons in the kitchen.
- Cooks should be rotated on a regular basis to avoid cooks staying too long in the kitchen. This may assist in reducing the malpractices in the kitchen. Also, prison warders should institute fair ways or criteria for selecting persons to work in the kitchen.
- Cooking and serving equipment should all have covers to ensure safety of food and should always be cleaned before and after cooking.
- Potatoes should be washed and peeled before cooking to improve the appearance of food.
- Vegetables should be washed, cut before cooking and cooked with oil rather than served separately.

Food Service
- Time of food served should be changed preferably, breakfast should be served at 7.00am, lunch at 12.00 and supper at 6.00pm to prevent prisoners staying long hours without food.

- Each prisoner should be provided personal individual utensils comprising a plate, cup and a spoon on admission to be surrendered on release.
- Food service areas and dining halls should be constructed for prisoners to take their meals to prevent elements of weather affecting food.
- Food should be served within 45 minutes of its preparation and not pre-served on plates long before eating time to prevent it from getting cold. Alternatively, installation of equipment that can retain heat or keep food warm should be considered.

Storage
- Stores should be renovated and partitioned to separate food and non-food items.
- Storage capacity of water should be increased to ensure that it is sufficient for all inmates hence improve hygiene and reduce diseases.

Kenya Prisons Service Department
- Drinking water should be treated or boiled.
- Civilianization of kitchen staff should be adopted instead of prisoners cooking and serving food through employment of civil servants to cook food as long as adequate security measures are put in place to prevent importation of drugs and other prohibited items into the prisons.
- Contract caterers should be considered in order to reduce use of food by kitchen personnel for trade and sexual favours of which standards can be dictated, maintained and monitored by the prisons.
- Employment of cateresses to manage food in prisons just like in learning institutions and have a catering department in the Prisons Headquarters to monitor catering practices and operations.
- Detergents and hot water should be provided for cleaning plates and equipment for food preparation and service.

- An examinable training programme should be developed for all prison wanders in-charge of kitchens.
- Training prison warders and storekeepers in catering discipline to enable them train prisoners attached to the kitchen.
- Prisoners should be trained on all areas of catering and be attached to institutions like schools under the community service order as part of their integration to society. This will not be a cost to the Prisons Department as the prisoners can be monitored by the institutions they are attached to and regular progress reports on the prisoners will be submitted. At the end of their term, the prisoners will have a career and in the process may help in reforming them. The kitchens can be used to train inmates in food production, to encourage them to seek employment on release. Courses can be structured, delivered, assessed, qualified and certificated to national standards. All training for prisoners can be acknowledged with an internationally recognized qualification that is acknowledged and accepted globally and can be an invaluable tool to securing employment on their return to society. These training standards can be quality assessed on an annual basis to ensure they meet the requirements laid down by the hospitality industry and the governing bodies of food safety. Successful training and accreditation of prisoners can reinforce positive behaviour that can eventually help in the reform process.

Government of Kenya
- Increase the budget allocation to prisons for the purchase of food, repairs and replacement of equipment and also renovations and maintenance of the kitchen.
- Food produced from the farms in prison should be used to feed the prisoners instead of selling all the farm produce then buying poor quality from contractors.

- Prisons should grow most of their own food in their farms to cut costs and assist in trying to provide a more nutritive diet.

Suggestions for Further Research

The researcher recommends the following for further research:

- Prisoners' nutritional needs, contents of meals and how these are identified and met.
- How good or bad flavour affects food intake, digestion and psychological well-being.
- The relationship between quality of catering services and costs implications.
- The mental, physical and spiritual effects of hunger.
- The extent to which purchasing, storage and distribution of food in prisons affect the quality of catering
- The relationship between quality of catering and behaviour of prisoners.

Appendices

Appendix I

Questionnaire for Prisoners

This questionnaire is to collect data for purely academic purposes. The study seeks to find out the factors affecting the quality of catering services in selected Prisons in Kenya. All information will be treated with strict confidence. Do not put any name or identification on this questionnaire.

Dear respondent,

There are six parts on the questionnaires, Part A, B, C, D, E and Part F. Kindly complete Part A on general information, Part B measures your expectations of the type of food in prison, Part C measures your perception on food preparation in prison, Part D measures your perception on food service in prison, Part E measures your perception on the challenges facing catering services in prisons and Part F measures your expectations on the overall quality of catering services in prison.

Please tick or fill in the blank spaces as appropriate.
Section A: Personal information
1. Age Below 25 yrs ☐ 26-30yrs ☐ 31-40 yrs ☐ Above 40 yrs ☐

2. Your Gender. Please tick.   Male ☐ Female ☐

3. Marital status. Married ☐   Single ☐
   Windowed ☐   Divorced ☐   Separated ☐

4. Highest level of education attained
   Form four (0-level) ☐ Form six (A-level) ☐College ☐
   University ☐ Primary ☐ Secondary ☐   None ☐

If College or University, Specify area of
specialization_____

5. What was your employment status before imprisonment?
   Employed ☐   Self-employed ☐   Unemployed ☐

6. What are your duties in prison?
   Carpentry ☐ Cooking ☐Masonry ☐ Manual ☐
   Jobs ☐ Welding ☐   Handwork ☐
   Household ☐   Dressmaking ☐
   Community ☐ Cleaning ☐

   Any other (specify) ——————————————————
   _____

7. Number of years in custody. Below 2 yrs ☐ 2-5 yrs ☐
   5 -10 yrs ☐   above 10 yrs ☐

8. Prior to your being imprisonment where were you living?
   In own house/home ☐ Self rented accommodation ☐
   Housed by Employers☐ Streets ☐
   Parents/Friend/Relatives ☐

   Other (specify)_____

9. Weight in Kgs:_____   Height. _____(m)
   BMI_____

10. Religion: Catholic ☐   Muslim ☐   Protestant ☐
    Other ☐

Section B: Type of food in prison

11. Please tick the food items you eat in prison and the frequency

	STATEMENT	Always	Very Often	Often	Rarely	Never
A	Maize	5	4	3	2	1
B	Beans	5	4	3	2	1
C	Soya flour	5	4	3	2	1
D	*Ndengu* (green grams)	5	4	3	2	1
E	Meat	5	4	3	2	1
F	Milk	5	4	3	2	1
G	Sugar	5	4	3	2	1
H	Salt	5	4	3	2	1
I	Vegetable oil or ghee	5	4	3	2	1
J	Green Vegetables	5	4	3	2	1
K	Carrots	5	4	3	2	1
L	Potatoes	5	4	3	2	1
M	Sweet Potatoes	5	4	3	2	1
N	Tomatoes	5	4	3	2	1
O	Onions	5	4	3	2	1
P	Capsicums	5	4	3	2	1
Q	***Ugali	5	4	3	2	1
R	***Porridge	5	4	3	2	1

Any   other   food   that   you   eat
(Specify)_____

12. How would you rate the following as pertains to the type of
food in prisoners? Please tick.

	STATEMENT	Very Good	Good	Average	Bad	Very Bad
A	Taste of the food	5	4	3	2	1
B	Odour of food	5	4	3	2	1
D	Texture of food	5	4	3	2	1
E	Colour of food	5	4	3	2	1
F	Appearance of the food	5	4	3	2	1
G	Nutritive value of food	5	4	3	2	1

13. How would you rate the following possible purposes of food in
prisons? Please tick.

	STATEMENT	Always	Very Often	Often	Rarely	Never
A	Reduced food as punishment	1	2	3	4	5
B	Increased food for sexual favours	1	2	3	4	5
C	Food as inducement e.g. Solicit information	1	2	3	4	5
D	Food for sustenance	1	2	3	4	5
G	No food as punishment	1	2	3	4	5

14. Are there any other reasons that can make a prisoner get more
or less food than the normal portion?   Yes ☐   No ☐

If yes, Specify_____

General rating of satisfaction on the quality of the type of food in prisons
Please circle the appropriate rating depending on the level of your
satisfaction with the quality of the type of food in prisons.

5. (Very satisfied)   4. (Satisfied) 3. (Slightly satisfied)
2. (Dissatisfied)   1. (Very dissatisfied)

Section C: Food preparation in prisons
15. How would you rate the following as pertains to food preparation
in prisons? Please tick.

	STATEMENT	Always	Very Often	Often	Rarely	Never
A	Reduced food as punishment	1	2	3	4	5
B	Increased food for sexual favours	1	2	3	4	5
C	Food as inducement e.g. Solicit information	1	2	3	4	5
D	Food for sustenance	1	2	3	4	5
G	No food as punishment	1	2	3	4	5

16. How would you rate the way persons are selected to prepare
food in your prison?

	STATEMENT	Always	Very Often	Often	Rarely	Never
A	Bad	1	2	3	4	5
B	Unfair	1	2	3	4	5
C	Favouritism	1	2	3	4	5
D	Corrupt	1	2	3	4	5
E	Commercial	1	2	3	4	5
F	As reward	1	2	3	4	5
G	Tribalism	1	2	3	4	5

Give any relevant comment on the persons cooking or their selection
....
17. a) Are special diets prepared in prison?   Yes ☐ No ☐

 b) If yes, when? Sick☐ Pregnant ☐ Breastfeeding ☐
Others (specify)_____

18. Is paraffin added to your food?   Yes ☐   No ☐

If yes, why do you think it is added_____

19. If no, do you think any other foreign substance is added to
    food? Yes ☐   No ☐
If yes please specify and explain why you think it is added to
food_____

*General rating on level of satisfaction on the quality of
preparation of food in prisons*
Please circle the appropriate one depending on the level of your
satisfaction with the quality of preparation of food in prisons.
5. (Very satisfied)   4. (Satisfied) 3. (Slightly satisfied)
2. (Dissatisfied)   1. (Very dissatisfied)

Section D: Food service in prisons
20. How would you rate the following as pertains to food service in
prisons? Please tick.

	STATEMENT	Very Good	Good	Average	Bad	Very Bad
A	The time food is served	5	4	3	2	1
B	Place of eating (environment)	5	4	3	2	1
C	Plates used	5	4	3	2	1
D	Mugs Used	5	4	3	2	1
E	Temperature of food	5	4	3	2	1
F	The persons serving the food	5	4	3	2	1
G	General hygiene of food service	5	4	3	2	1
H	The quantity of food served	5	4	3	2	1
I	The equipment used to serve food	5	4	3	2	1

21. How would you rate the way persons are selected to serve food
in your prison?

	STATEMENT	Always	Very Often	Often	Rare
A	Bad	1	2	3	4
B	Unfair	1	2	3	4
C	Favouritism	1	2	3	4
D	Corrupt	1	2	3	4
E	Commercial	1	2	3	4
F	As reward	1	2	3	4
G	Tribalism	1	2	3	4

Give any relevant comment on the persons cooking or their selection
....

22. Are you provided with water to wash hands before eating?
     Yes ☐   No ☐

23. Have you ever been sick because of food? Tick as applicable.
  1. Severally ☐   2. Very often ☐   3. Often ☐
  4. Rarely ☐   5. Never ☐

If you have been sick, please state the illness_____

General rating on the level of satisfaction on the quality of food service in prisons
Please circle the appropriate one depending on the level of your satisfaction with the quality of food service in prisons.
5. (Very satisfied)   4. (Satisfied)   3. (Slightly satisfied)
2. (Dissatisfied)   1. (Very dissatisfied)

Section E: View of prison mgt on catering service in prison
23. Indicate the rating of the prison management towards ensuring good catering practices in respect to the following

	STATEMENT	Very Good	Good	Average	Poor	Very Poor
A	Temperature of food	5	4	3	2	1
B	Hygienic conditions of food service	5	4	3	2	1
C	Equality of food served	5	4	3	2	1
D	Time of food service	5	4	3	2	1
E	Method of food service	5	4	3	2	1

24. How much influence does the food have on your behavior? (please tick)

None	Very little	Unsure	Some	A lot

If it has some or a lot of influence, please specify how

_____

_____

25. Do you think the conditions of prison food can make prisoners want to stay in prison?

Yes ☐   No ☐

Please explain your answer_____

26. Do you receive food from anywhere else other than the prison food?   Yes ☐   No ☐

If yes, specify_____

27. What comments can you make as far as catering practices in prisons is concerned?

....

....

28. What recommendations can you make to improve the catering in prisons?

....

....

Section F: Overall rating on the level of satisfaction on the quality of catering in prisons

Please circle the appropriate rating on the overall level of your satisfaction with the quality of catering in prisons. Compared to how satisfied I expect to be with the quality of catering in prisons, I find that I am:

5. (Very satisfied)   4. (Satisfied)   3. (Slightly satisfied)
2. (Dissatisfied)   1. (Very dissatisfied)

END OF QUESTIONNAIRE
Thank You for taking your time to fill in the questionnaire

Appendix II

Interview schedule for warders

This questionnaire is to collect data for purely academic purposes. The study seeks to find out the factors affecting the quality of catering services in selected Prisons in Kenya. All information will be treated with strict confidence. Do not put any name or identification on this questionnaire.

Name of Prison:_____

Please tick or fill in the blank spaces as appropriate

Section A: Personal information
1. Age ☐ Below 25 yrs ☐ 26-30yrs ☐
   31-40 yrs ☐ Above 40 yrs ☐

2. Your Gender. Please tick. Male ☐ Female ☐

3. Marital status. Married ☐ Single ☐ Windowed ☐
   Divorced ☐ Separated ☐

4. Highest level of education attained
   Primary ☐ Non ☐
   Form four (0-level) ☐ Form six (A-level) ☐
   College ☐ University ☐

If   College   or   University,   Specify   area   of
specialization_____

5. Do you have any training in catering or handling food?
Yes ☐   No ☐

6. Specify your job title _____

7. Number of years in service   Below 5 yrs
5 - 10 yrs ☐   above 10 yrs ☐

8. Where do you live?   Employer ☐   Rented house ☐
With parents/Relatives ☐ Other ☐

Section B: Type of food

Please tick the relevant answers
1. What do you think about the type of food served in prisons?
Please tick.

	STATEMENT	Very Good	Good	Average	Bad	Very Bad
A	The type of food in prison	5	4	3	2	1
B	The quantity of food	5	4	3	2	1
C	Taste of the food	5	4	3	2	1
D	Odour of food	5	4	3	2	1
E	Texture of food	5	4	3	2	1
F	Colour of food	5	4	3	2	1
G	Nutritive value of food	5	4	3	2	1
H	Appearance of the food	5	4	3	2	1

2. Are there special diets served to prisoners?

Yes ☐   No ☐

If yes, when?   Sick   Pregnant   Breastfeeding   Other
Specify any others_____

Section C: Food service

3. To what extend do you experience the following problems in service of food? Please rate

	STATEMENT	Always	V. Often	Often	Rarely	Never
A	Inadequate serving equipment	1	2	3	4	5
B	Large number of prisoners to serve	1	2	3	4	5
C	Long queues	1	2	3	4	5
D	Ensuring equal quantities for all	1	2	3	4	5
E	Poor method of service	1	2	3	4	5
F	Place of serving food not conducive	1	2	3	4	5
G	Poor temperature of food served	1	2	3	4	5
H	Inadequate plates	1	2	3	4	5

Any other problems (Specify).......................................
....

Section D: Food production

4. To what extend are the following problems encountered in food production? Please tick

	STATEMENT	Always	V. Often	Often	Rarely	Never
A	Lack of adequate equipment	1	2	3	4	5
B	Poor/ Low quality of ingredients	1	2	3	4	5
C	Inadequate ingredients	1	2	3	4	5
D	Lack of adequate source of energy	1	2	3	4	5
E	Difficulties in preparing large quantities of food	1	2	3	4	5
F	Untrained cooks	1	2	3	4	5
G	Inadequate kitchen space	1	2	3	4	5

Any other problems (Specify).......................................
....
.

5. How are inmates selected to do cooking and service? Please tick.

	STATEMENT	YES	NO
A	Behaviour		
B	Qualifications		
C	Reward		
D	Tribalism		
E	Nepotism		
F	Religion		
G	Age		
H	Favoritism		
I	Length of stay in prison		

6. Do you have any measures in place to ensure all inmates get food? Yes   No

If yes (specify) _____

_____

7. If catering services are improved, do you think it can help in the reform prisoners? Yes/No

Please explain your answer _____

8. If catering services are improved, do you think it can make prisoners enjoy being in prison hence increase crime rate   Yes   No

Please explain your answer _____

_____

9. a) Are there situations where prisoners are denied or given more food for different reasons? Yes/No

b   If yes, Specify the situations ....

10. How much influence does the food have on the behaviour of prisoners? (please tick)

None	Very little	Unsure	Some	A lot

Please explain your answer _____

_____

_____

11.   What suggestions can you make in regard to catering services offered in prisons

_____

_____

_____

_____

_____

_____

_____

12.   Make recommendations on how you think the catering services in prisons can be improved

_____

_____

_____

_____

_____

_____

_____

Section E: Overall rating on the level of satisfaction on the quality of catering in prisons

Please circle the appropriate one depending on the level of your satisfaction with the quality of catering in prisons. Compared to how satisfied I expect to be with the quality of catering in prisons, I find that I am:

5. (Very satisfied)   4. (Satisfied) 3. (Slightly satisfied)
   2. (Dissatisfied) 1. (Very dissatisfied)

END OF QUESTIONNAIRE
Thanks for taking your time to fill in the questionnaire

Appendix III

Interview Schedule for Storekeepers

This questionnaire is to collect data for purely academic purposes. The study seeks to find out the factors affecting the quality of catering services in selected Prisons in Kenya. All information will be treated with strict confidence. Do not put any name or identification on this questionnaire.

Name of Prison:_____

Please tick or fill in the blank spaces as appropriate

Section A: Personal information

1. Age ☐   Below 25 yrs ☐   26-30yrs ☐

    31-40 yrs ☐   Above 40 yrs ☐

2. Your Gender. Please tick.   Male ☐   Female ☐

3. Marital status. Married ☐ Single ☐   Windowed ☐

    Divorced ☐   Separated ☐

4. Highest level of education attained
    Form four (0-level) ☐   Form six (A-level) ☐

College ☐   University ☐

Primary ☐   Non ☐

If College or University, Specify area of specialization_____

5. Do you have any training in storekeeping? Yes ☐   No ☐

6. Specify your job title _____

7. Number of years in service
   Below 5 yrs ☐   5 - 10 yrs ☐   above 10 yrs ☐

8. Where do you live? Employer ☐   Rented house ☐
   With parents/Relatives ☐   Other ☐

Section B: Purchasing of food
13. Please explain the procedure for purchasing food supplies.

_____

_____

14. Who is responsible for food purchases?_____

15. Is the amount of food received enough to cater for all prisoners?
YES / NO

16. How do you ensure that there will be adequate food incase of a sudden increase in prisoners?

_____

17.   How do you ensure quality of the food received?

_____

_____

18.   Do you ever run out of supplies? YES / NO

19.   Please tick the food you receive in the store and the frequency.

	STATEMENT	Always	Very Often	Often	Rarely	Never
A	Maize	5	4	3	2	1
B	Beans	5	4	3	2	1
C	Soya flour	5	4	3	2	1
D	*Ndengu* (green grams)	5	4	3	2	1
E	Meat	5	4	3	2	1
F	Milk	5	4	3	2	1
G	Sugar	5	4	3	2	1
H	Salt	5	4	3	2	1
I	Vegetable oil or ghee	5	4	3	2	1
J	Green Vegetables	5	4	3	2	1
K	Carrots	5	4	3	2	1
L	Potatoes	5	4	3	2	1
M	Sweet Potatoes	5	4	3	2	1
N	Maize for flour	5	4	3	2	1

20. What do you think about the type of food received in prisons? Please tick.

	STATEMENT	Very Good	Good	Average	Bad	Very Bad
A	The quantity of food	5	4	3	2	1
B	Appearance of the food items	5	4	3	2	1
C	Colour of food items	5	4	3	2	1
D	Freshness of food items	5	4	3	2	1

21. Are there special food received for preparation of special diets to prisoners?   Yes ☐   No ☐

If yes, Specify any others _____

_____

22. What challenges do you face in purchasing food?

_____

_____

Section C: Storage

23. Are there any storage facilities? YES / NO

24. Please explain the procedures of storing food supplies.

_____

_____

25. What problems do you encounter in the storage of food?

_____

_____

26. To what extend do you experience the following problems in storage of food? Please rate

	STATEMENT	Always	V. Often	Often	Rarely	Never
A	Space	1	2	3	4	5
B	Temperature	1	2	3	4	5

Any other problems (Specify) ....

Section D: Distribution of food

27. How is food distributed?

_____

28. How do you measure the amount of food to be released?

_____

29. How do you ensure that the food from the store is used entirely by the prisons?

_____

30. To what extend are the following problems encountered in distribution of food? Please tick

	STATEMENT	Always	V. Often	Often	Rarely	Never
A	Lack of supplies	1	2	3	4	5
B	Poor/Low quality of ingredients	1	2	3	4	5
C	Inadequate ingredients	1	2	3	4	5

Any other problems (Specify)......................................
....
31. Do you think the stores department affects the quality of food service and production? YES/NO
Please explain your answer _____

_____

32. Make recommendations on how you think storekeeping operations can improve quality of catering services in prisons.

_____

_____

_____

_____

_____

_____

_____

_____

_____

_____

_____

_____

Section E: Overall rating on the Level of Satisfaction on the quality of store items in prisons

Please circle the appropriate one depending on the level of your satisfaction with the quality of food in the store in prisons. Compared to how satisfied I expect to be with the quality of food in prisons, I find that I am:

5. (Very satisfied)   4. (Satisfied)   3. (Slightly satisfied)

2. (Dissatisfied)   1. (Very dissatisfied)

END OF QUESTIONNAIRE

Thanks for taking your time to fill in the questionnaire

Appendix IV

Interview schedule for Officers-In-Charge

This questionnaire is to collect data for purely academic purposes. The study seeks to find out the factors affecting the quality of catering services in selected Prisons in Kenya. All information will be treated with strict confidence. Do not put any name or identification on this questionnaire.

Name of Prison:_____

Please tick or fill in the blank spaces as appropriate

Section A: Personal information

1. Age Below 25 yrs ☐   26-30yrs ☐

   31-40 yrs ☐   Above 40 yrs ☐

2. Your Gender. Please tick. Male ☐   Female ☐

3. Marital status. Married ☐ Single ☐   Windowed ☐

   Divorced ☐   Separated ☐

4. Highest level of education attained: Form four ☐
   Form six ☐   College ☐   University ☐
   Primary ☐   Non ☐

If College or University, Specify area of specialization_____

---

6. Number of years in service Below   5 yrs ☐

   5 - 10 yrs ☐   above 10 yrs ☐

7. Where do you live? Employer ☐   Rented house ☐

   With parents/Relatives ☐   Other ☐

Section B: Type of food
1. What is your view about the type of food served in prisons?

_____

_____

2. Please tick the food items ordered by the management in prison.

	FOOD	YES	NO
A	Maize		
B	Beans		
C	Soya flour		
D	*Ndengu* (green grams)		
E	Meat		
F	Milk		
G	Sugar		
H	Salt		
I	Vegetable oil or ghee		
J	Green Vegetables		
K	Carrots		
L	Potatoes		
M	Sweet Potatoes		

3. For items not ordered in no. 2, what problems do you face in receiving them?

_____

_____

4. Are you satisfied with the type of food given to prisoners?
YES / NO

Section C: Food service

1. Are you satisfied with the way food is served?   YES / NO

2. What challenges are faced in food service?

_____

_____

Section D: Food production

33.   Are you satisfied with food preparation in prisons?
YES / NO

34.   What challenges are faced in food preparation?

_____

_____

35.   If catering services are improved, do you think it can help in reforming prisoners? Yes/ No
Please explain your answer_____

_____

_____

36.   If catering services are improved, do you think it can make prisoners enjoy being in prison hence increase crime rate
Yes ☐   No ☐
Please explain your answer _____

_____

_____

37.   a) Are there situations where prisoners are denied or given more food for different reasons? Yes/No
b   If yes, Specify the situations ....
....

38. How much influence do you think food has on the behaviour of
    prisoners? (please tick)

None	Very little	Unsure	Some	A lot

Please explain your answer _____

39.   Do you think there is need to improve catering in prisons?
YES / NO

40.   Do you think the amount allocated to your prison is adequate?
YES / NO

41.   Make recommendations on how you think the catering
services in prisons can be improved

_____
_____
_____

Section E: Overall rating on the level of satisfaction on the quality of catering in prisons

Please circle the appropriate one depending on the level of your
satisfaction with the quality of catering in prisons. Compared to how
satisfied I expect to be with the quality of catering in prisons, I find
that I am:

5. (Very satisfied)   4. (Satisfied)   3. (Slightly satisfied)   2.
(Dissatisfied) 1. (Very dissatisfied)

END OF QUESTIONNAIRE
Thanks for taking your time to fill in the questionnaire

Appendix V

Observation schedule

The following questions will guide the researcher & research assistants during observation.

Name of Prison_____ Date_____Day of the week _____ Meal: B.L.S.

1. Describe the type of cooking equipment used

_____

2. Take note of the type of food served and the time served

Meal	Time Served	Specific food
Breakfast		
Lunch		
Supper		

3. Indicate the methods of food preparation used

_____

4. Examine the methods of service used

_____

_____

5. Measure the temperature of food:

After cooking	Before service	1st Service	1/3rd Service	2/3rd Service	Last Serving

6. Describe the persons preparing food.

_____

7. Describe the service persons

_____

8. Describe the conditions of the dining area

_____

9. Describe the state of the plates used   (Clean, Dirty, Old, New, Good, Bad)

_____

10. Observe if the quantities of food served is equal to all prisoners

_____

11. Examine if the food quantity is enough for prisoners

_____

12. Note the measurement used for the quantity of food and drink

_____

13. Comment on the storage facilities

_____

14. Observe the quality of ingredients used in food preparation

_____

15. Describe the hygiene of the food preparation area

_____

16.   Note the time food is prepared- B/Fast_____
Lunch_____ Supper_____

17. Please note and explain any relevant observations made.

_____
_____
_____
_____

18. What recommendations can be made to improve catering in this prison.

_____
_____

Appendix VI

Authority letter to collect data

OFFICE OF THE VICE PRESIDENT AND MINISTRY OF HOME AFFAIRS

KENYA PRISONS SERVICE

Jacqueline Korir
Moi University
School of Business and Management
Dept. of Hotel & Hospitality Management
P O Box 1125
ELDORET

RE: DATA COLLECTION - RESEARCH ON INVESTIGATION ON THE QUALITY OF CATERING IN SELECTED PRISONS IN KENYA

As per the request of Moi University on your behalf regarding the above-mentioned subject, the Commissioner of Prisons has granted you permission to carry out the research. You should liaise with the officers in charge of the prisons mentioned. They (officers in charge) will ensure that you have a uniformed officer during the exercise.

Looking forward to working with you.

Dr. J. C. KIBOSIA - DIRECTOR (PRISONS HEALTH SERVICES)
For: COMMISSIONER OF PRISONS

cc The Commissioner of Prisons

SDLP

Head - Research/Statistics/Insp. Unit

O/Cs - Eldoret Main and Women Prisons, Kisumu Main and Women Prisons, Kapsabet Prison, Kericho Main and Women Prisons, Kamiti Prison, Langata Women and Ngeria Prison

Appendix VII

Authority letter to take photographs

E. Hand M

(49)

OFFICE OF THE VICE PRESIDENT AND MINISTRY OF HOME AFFAIRS
KENYA PRISONS SERVICE

COMMISSIONE

PRISONS HEADQUARTERS
P.O. BOX 30175-00100
NAIROBI

Date:

The Officer In Charge:

Kamiti Main

Langata Women

Eldoret Main

Eldoret Women

Ngeria Prison

PHOTOGRAPHS FOR RESEARCH WORK

The Commissioner of Prisons has authorized bearing Karir of Moi University to take above. You should determine appropriately areas relevant to research.

Dr. J. C. KIBOSIA
For: COMMISSIONER OF PRISONS

C.C.

CP

SCCP

References

Allyson, C. and Burns, H. *Prison conditions in the United Kingdom*. New York: Human Rights Watch, 2005.

Amnesty International Equatorial Guinea. "Prisoners face death by starvation." IRINWA Report 3-3, 15th Apr. 2005: 272. Amnesty international Kenya. "Prisons: Deaths due to torture and cruel, inhuman and degrading conditions." [on-line] Available at http://web.amnesty.org/8../5D06B274292A699E802569AE0052D591! Open&Highlight=2,keny, 2000.

Ananova: "Prison food too good to eat." http://www.ananova.com/news/story/ sm_ 2384948.html. Accessed on 18th July, 2008.

Barton, P. "Government Regulation of the Integrity of the Food Supply 4." *ANN-REV of Nutrition*. 1-3 (1994): 1-20

Beaton, G. H. "Approaches to analysis of dietary data: Relationship between planned analyses and choice of methodology." *American Journal of Clinical Nutrition* 59 (1994): 253S - 261S, 18-22

Beaton *et al*. Appropriate uses of anthropometric indices in children. A report based on an ACC/SCN workshop. New York. ACC/SCN Nutrition Policy Discussion Paper No. 7: 51, 1990.

Beckford, J. and Gilliat, S. *Religion in prison: Equal rites in a m u l t i - faith society*. Cambridge: Cambridge University Press, 1998.

Bell, J. *Doing your Research Project*.3rd Ed. Bunkigham: Open University Press, 1999.

Bosworth, M. F. *Encyclopedia of Prisons and Correctional Facilities*. California: Sage Publications, 2004.

Bourn, J: Head of NAO. "Quality and cost of prison catering: report by the controller & Auditor General. London: NAO: 1-2, 1997.

Brown, D. R. and Henkel, S. L. *The non-commercial Food Service Manager's Handbook: A complete guide to Hospitals, Nursing Homes, Military, Prisons, Schools and Churches*. London: Atlantic Publishing, 2006.

Burton-Rose, Pens, D., and Wright, P. *The celling of America: An inside look at the U.S. prison industry.* Monroe: Common Courage, 1998.

Butunyi, C and Siele, S. "Jail transfers halt in war on cholera." The Daily Nation 23 Mar. 2009:6.

Carlson, P. M and Garett, J. S. *Prison and Jail Administration: Practice and Theory.* 2nd Ed. London: Jones and Bartlett, 1999.

Chabari P. and Kibosia J. "The Development of Prisons Service." Health Services Unit-Concept and Preliminary Proposal. Kenya Prisons Service Department, Nairobi, 2007

Chibvuri, Bright. 'Pathetic Prison Conditions'. An Africa News r e p o r t Oct. 1997: 2-4.

"Cholera outbreaks in Kenyan Prisons". http://www.afriquejet.com/news/ africa-news/kenya %e2%80%99s-cholera-outbreak- spreads-from- prisons,-31-killed-2009032724466.html. Accessed on 18th August, 2008.

Davis, Lockwood, A., and Stone, S. *Food and Beverage Management.* Oxford: Elsevier Butterworth- Heinemann, 1998.

Donovan, W. "Prison Food not Fancy." New Jersey: Fight club, 19th Dec. 1982.

Dudek, S. G. *Nutrition Essentials for Nursing Practice.* 5th Ed. Philadelphia: Lippincott W. &W. 2006.

Edwards J. S. A. *et a.l,* eds. "The nutritional content of male prisoners' diet in the UK." *Journal of Human Nutrition and Dietetics* 1 (2001) : 25-33

Ekwuruke, H. *"The Dehumanizing Conditions of Detainees in Nigerian Prisons".* Abuja: Panorama, 2005.

Flynn, N. and Douglas, H. *Introduction to Prisons and Imprisonment: Prison reform trust.* Winchester: Waterside Press, 1998.

Fraenkel, J. and Warren, N. *Reliability in Research Instruments: A Concept Note.* Paris: New-way Publishers, 2000.

Glenna, G. "Living with HIV in Uganda's Prison Cells." Monitor Publications, 25th May. 2008: 5

Greenwood, A. "Taste-Testing Nutraloaf: The Prison Food that just might be unconstitutionally Bad." Slate Magazine 24th June. 2008: 1-3

Godderis, R. "Food in Prison." *The Howard Journal Vol 45 No 3. July 2006 ISSN 0265-5527.* D.Phil Thesis. University of Calgary, Canada. 255-267.

"Harsh Prison conditions in Kenya."http://asiapacific.amnesty. org/library/ index/ ENGAFR 320122001. Accessed on 14th July, 2008.

Harerimana, F.M: Minister for internal security, Rwanda. "Government Bans

Bringing Food for Prisoners". Hirondelle News Agency: 26th June: 8, 2008.

http://www.country-data.com/cgi_bin/query/r-9483.html. Accessed on 24th July, 2008.

Jablonsky, S.and De Vries, D. 'Operant conditioning principles extrapolated to the theory of management', in *Organisational Behaviour and Human Performance*, 14, 1972.

Johnson, E. "Lunch at Lizira Prison". Scarlett Lion. 5 July. 2008: 2

Johnson, R. and Bhattacharyya, G. *Statistics: principles and methods*. New York: John Wiley & Sons Inc, 1987.

Jones, P. *Food Service Operations*. 2nd Ed. London: Cassell Educational Limited, 1988.

Karanja, N. et al. "Cholera kills prisoner, 12 others in hospital." The Standard Newspaper 24 March. 2009:9.

Kenya, Ministry of Finance, Central Bureau of Statistics (CBS). *"National micro and small enterprise base line survey."* Nairobi: Government Printers, 1999.

Kenya, Ministry of Health.*"Kenya National Guidelines on Nutrition and HIV/AIDS."* Nairobi: Government Printers, 2007.

Kerlinger, F. N. *Foundations of Behavioral Research*. New York: Surjeet Publications, 1978.

Kinton, R., Ceserani, V., and Foskett, D. *Theory of Catering*. London: Hodder Education, 2002.

Korane: Nyeri District Commissioner. "Prison conditions in Kenya." Daily Nation 21 Sept. 2000: 12.

Kothari, C. R. *Research methodology: Methods and techniques*. 2nd Ed. New Delhi: New Age International (P) Ltd, 2008.

Koutsoyiannis, A. *Theory of Ergonometrics*. London: Macmillan Press, 1993.

Labo, H. S: Assistant to Nigeria's Prison Inspector. "Nigeria in overcrowded prisons: survival is a daily battle." IRIN, 11 Jan. 2006:3.

Last Alex, "The notorious jails of Nigeria". Lagos: BBC News – 7th April 2006.

Lausanne, D. "Rwanda Government Bans Bringing Food for Prisoners." *World news journal* 10 (2008): 8.

Laws of Kenya. The Prisons Act, Chapter 90. Nairobi: Government Printer, 2008.

Marquart, J. W. and Roebuck, J. B. "Institutional Control and the Christmas Festival in a Maximum Security Penitentiary." Urban Life, 3/4(January 1987): 449-473.

Mugenda, M. O. and Mugenda, A. G. *Research Methods Quantitative and Qualitative Approaches.* Nairobi: ACTS Press, 1999.

Mutai, L. M . *Qualitative Research Approaches: The Modern Perspective.* New Delhi: Oaklands, 2001.

"Nakuru prison inmate latest cholera victim." Daily Nation, 24 Mar. 2009: 23.

National Audit Office. "HM Prison Service, Prison Catering. Report by the Comptroller and Auditor General". London: The Stationery Office, 1997.

National Audit Office report."Serving Time: Prisoner Diet and Exercise." London: The Stationery Office, 2006.

Neuman, L. *Research Methods: Qualitative and Quantitative Approaches.* Oakland: Sage Publications, 2000.

New Zealand Qualifications Authority. "Supervise and monitor standards of catering operations and staff in food services." http://www.moh.govt.nz/. Accessed on 20th January, 2009.

"Nigerian Prisons." http://news.bbc.co.uk/2/hi/africa/4880592.stm Accessed on 24th July, 2008.

Ogbozor, E. "Punishment and Crime" Prisoners Rehabilitation and Welfare Action. Lagos: IRIN, 2006.

O'Hare, K. R. "Prison Food, Clothing, Education, and R e c r e a t i o n ." Excerpts from Chapter 6 in, Sometime Federal prisoner number 21669 (New York: Alfred A. Knopf, 1923): 86-97, 2006.

Ombudsman. Northern Ireland Annual Report: 14, 2008.

Oswaldo, P."Inhuman Conditions of Cuban Prisons." *Havana Journal, Cuba forum*: (5th August, 2008).

Paige, M.H and Beck, A.J. Prison and Jail Inmates at Midyear 2004. London: Bureau of Justice statistics: 2, 2005.

Parasuraman, A., Zeithaml, and Berry, L. *Delivering Quality Service.* New York: Free Press, 1990.

Patton, M. *Quantitative and Qualitative Research Approaches.* London: Prentice Hall, 2002.

Peil, M. *Research Methods: A handbook for Africa.* Nairobi: EAEP, 1995.

Pens, D. "Food strike puts Washington DOC on spin control". P r i s o n Legal News 2001: 9

Phinney, D. *Contract Meals Disaster for Iraqi Prisoners*. Iowa: Oakland, 2004.

Reform International. "Ninety prisoners die each month in Kenya Prison." Daily Nation, 12 June 2000: 9.

Ruzbeh, N. B. and Bedi, K. *Shadows in Cages: Mother and Child in Indian Prisons*. Himalayan: Diamond Pocket Books, 2004.

Sanchez, E. J. Look Beyond Capital Punishment. 26 Nov. 1994: 12-16.

Scanlon, N. L. *Catering Management*. 3rd Ed. New Jersey: John Wiley & Sons Inc, 2008.

Sethi, M. *Institutional Food Management*. New Delhi: New Age International Publishers, 2008.

Skinner, B. F. *About Behaviorism*. Random House, 1974.

Smith, C. "Punishment and pleasure: women, food and the imprisoned body." *The Howard Journal* 39-4 (2002) :339–353. *The Sociological Review*, 50 (2002): 197–214

Wanjohi G. J. "Prison conditions In Kenya." *A Journal of Social and Religious Concern*. 12-4 (1997):1-6

West, A. Walker, A. Lawson, J. 'Effects of food processing in hospital catering systems. In: Edwards J & L.Ross (ed) Culinary Arts and Sciences. Global and National Perspectives". Bournemouth: Worshipful Company of Cook Centre. 1998: 283-289

Whitney, E. N. and Rolfes, S.R. *Understanding Nutrition*. 9th Ed. Ohio: Wadsworth, 2002.

Wyke, N. "Italian Prison Food-an insider guide." Times Online 2007: 17-21

Young, J and Jaspers, S. *The Meaning and Measurement of Acute Malnutrition in Emergencies. A primer for Decision Makers*. London: Overseas Development Institute, 2006.

"Zimbabwe Prisoners forced to go without food." Harare: 12th June 2006: 24.

The Quality of Catering in Kenyan Prisons

Index

Index of Personal Names

Index of Subjects

Auditing Priniples: A Stuents' Handbook by Musa O. Nyakora (2007) *The Concept of* Botho *and HIV/AIDS in Botswana* edited by Joseph B. R. Gaie and Sana K. MMolai (2007)

Captive of Fate: A Novel by Ketty Arucy (2007)

A Guide to Ethics by Joseph Njino (2008)

Pastoral Theology: Rediscovering African Models and Methods by Ndung'u John Brown Ikenye (2009)

The Royal Son: Balancing Barthian and African Christologies by Zablon Bundi Mutongu (2009)

AIDS, Sexuality, and Gender: Experiencing of Women in Kenyan Universities by Nyokabi Kamau (2009)

Modern Facilitation and Training Methodology: A Guide to Best Practice in Africa by Frederick Chelule (2009)

How to Write a Winning Thesis by Simon Kang'ethe et al (2009)

Absolute Power and Other Stories by Ambrose Rotich Keitany (2009)

Y'sdom in Africa: A Personal Journey by Stanley Kinyeki (2010)

Abortion and Morality Debate in Africa: A Philosophical Enquiry by George Kegode (2010)

The Holy Spirit as Liberator: A Study of Luke 4: 14-30 by Joseph Koech (2010)

Biblical Studies, Theology, Religion and Philosophy: An Introduction for African Universities, Gen. Ed. James N. Amanze (2010)

Modeling for Servant-Leaders in Africa: Lessons from St. Paul by Ndung'u John Brown Ikenye (2010)

HIV & AIDS, Communication and Secondary Education in Kenya By Ndeti Ndati (2011)

Disability, Society and Theology: Voices from Africa By Samuel Kabue et al (2011)

If You Have No Voice Just Sing!: Narratives of Women's Lives and Theological Education at St. Paul's University By Esther Mombo And Heleen Joziasse (2011)

Mutira Mission: An African Church Comes of Age in Kirinyaga, Kenya (1912-2012) By Julius Gathogo (2011)

The Bible and African Culture: Mapping Transactional Inroads By Humphrey Waweru, (2011)

Karl Jaspers' Philosophy of Existence: Insights for Out Time By Cletus N. Chukwu (2011)

www.ingramcontent.com/pod-product-compliance
Lightning Source LLC
Chambersburg PA
CBHW022316280326
41932CB00010B/1118